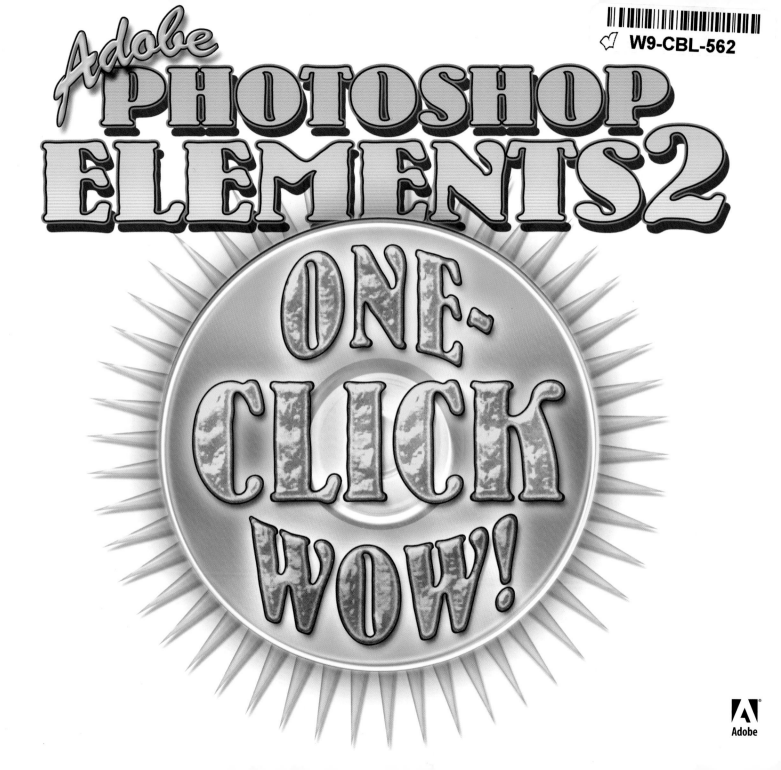

Adobe Photoshop Elements 2 One-Click Wow!

Jack Davis

Peachpit Press / Adobe Press
1249 Eighth Street
Berkeley, CA 94710
(510) 524-2178
(510) 524-2221 (fax)

Find us on the World Wide Web at:
www.peachpit.com/wow

Peachpit Press is a division of Pearson Education
Adobe Photoshop Elements 2 One-Click Wow! is published in association with Adobe Press

To report errors, please send a note to errata@peachpit.com

Copyright © 2004 by Jack Davis and Linnea Dayton

Cover design: Jack Davis

Book design: Jill Davis

Production and prepress: Jonathan Parker

Direct-to-plate printing: CDS / Medford, Oregon

ISBN 0-321-16888-7

0 9 8 7 6 5 4 3 2 1

Printed and bound in the United States of America

To Linnea ...

— Jack

ACKNOWLEDGMENTS

As always, I had a great deal of help with putting this book and CD-ROM together. First, I personally want to acknowledge Linnea Dayton, my partner of over 10 years. Though she was not involved in this specific version of *One-Click Wow!* her expertise is evident thoughout, due to her work on previous editions. I also want to thank the friends and family of both Linnea and myself who let us "style" some of their photos to help illustrate the pages. And my thanks go to Piper Carr and others at Corbis Images who allowed us to use photos from their Royalty Free collections when my own just wouldn't fill the bill.

Several people helped make sure this CD-and-book package communicates clearly: I am especially grateful to my wonderful wife Jill Davis for designing the book; to Garen Checkley for beta-testing and copy-editing; to Cher Threinen-Pendarvis for beta-testing and proofreading, and to Jonathan Parker for producing the pages and preparing them for printing.

I'd also like to thank the many supporters at Peachpit Press — in particular, my publisher Nancy Ruenzel, editor Cary Norsworthy, production coordinator Connie Jeung-Mills, technical-expert Victor Gavenda and especially media producer Heidi Jonk-Sommer, who did invaluable and extensive manuscript/CD testing.

Finally, thanks to all who have helped with nine editions of *The Photoshop Wow! Book.* The experience that was gained in that project has made *Adobe Photoshop Elements 2 One-Click Wow!* possible, and I'm delighted to pass it on.

CONTENTS

HOW TO USE THIS BOOK & CD-ROM

Read the book for pointers on applying and customizing the One-Click Wow! Presets on the CD-ROM.

▶ *Throughout the book are tips in this format — starting with an orange pointer to catch your eye. The tips provide useful information about working in Adobe Photoshop Elements 2. Here are some topics and tips you may find especially useful:*

- *A Quick Start Guide to installing and using the Wow Presets (pages 2–3)*
- *What is a Layer Style? (pages 6–7)*
- *Scaling and Customizing applied Styles (pages 9–11)*
- *Saving, Sizing and Outputting your finished image (pages 15–17)*

The *Adobe Photoshop Elements 2 One-Click Wow!* book-and-CD-ROM package brings you the following:

On the CD-ROM —

- **More than 500 sophisticated Layer Styles** (offering thousands of possible combinations) for enhancing your photos, type, and artwork
- "Before," "During," and "After" **One-Click Wow! Layer Style Tutorial files** for practicing all aspects of working with Styles
- A **layered "One-Click Wow Test" file including a photo and graphics** you can use to practice applying or storing Styles that you customize yourself and want to save and use again
- **Forty Gradient presets** you can use in Gradient Fill layers or with the Gradient tool to make backgrounds or multicolor tints
- A working **try-out version of Adobe Photoshop Elements 2**

In the book —

- Turn to **"One-Click Wow! Quick Start"** on pages 2–3 to learn how to load the Styles, prepare your file, and **apply a Style**.
- The **"Layer Style 'Magic'"** section, starting on page 8, begins by demonstrating how flexible and easy-to-use Styles are. Also included in this section are tips for **"Scaling a Style"** once you've applied it (pages 9–10); **"Customizing Style Settings"** for modifying a Style (page 11); **"Combining Styles"** to remove, replace, or add effects by applying another Style (page 12); **"Copying a Layer Style"** to apply customized or combined Styles to other photos, type, or graphics (page 13); **"Using Styles with Clipping Groups"** for "styling" images "framed" within a shape or type (page 14).

- **"Saving, Sizing & Output"** (pages 15–17) shows you how to make a file the right size and format for printing, posting on the Web, or attaching to an email.
- **"A Layer Style Tutorial"** (pages 18–21) walks you through applying, customizing, and copying and pasting Styles, as well as making changes to layer content after a Style is applied, using the **Tutorial files** provided on the CD-ROM.
- Pages 26–77 show printed applications and samples of the Layer Styles on the CD. These examples are organized in two sections — **"Styles for Photos"** (pages 26–45), and **"Styles for Type and Graphics"** (pages 46–77).
- **Section 4** of the book (pages 78–89) shows you how to use the other Wow Presets — **Wow Media Brushes**, **Wow Patterns**, and **Wow Gradients**.

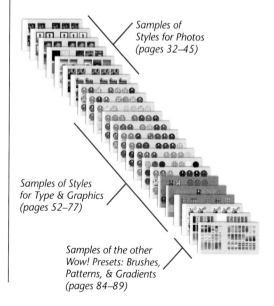

Samples of Styles for Photos (pages 32–45)

Samples of Styles for Type & Graphics (pages 52–77)

Samples of the other Wow! Presets: Brushes, Patterns, & Gradients (pages 84–89)

ONE-CLICK WOW! QUICK START

Can't wait to get started? Here's how to get going right away.

▶ *One of the benefits of using Layer Styles is that they are just as easy to "un-apply" — leaving your image untouched — as they are to apply in the first place. But if you also plan to experiment with an image in a way that could compromise the original, it's a good idea to duplicate the image before you start working in Elements. That way you can work on the duplicate and still have the untouched original for safekeeping. After you open the file (File > Open), choose* **Image > Duplicate Image and click OK** *in the Duplicate Image dialog box.*

To install and use the **One-Click Wow! Presets**, you'll need to **first install** Adobe® Photoshop® Elements 2. (There's a try-out version of Elements 2 on the **One-Click Wow! CD-ROM.**) If you need help with the installation process, check the instructions that came with the program. Once it's installed, follow the numbered steps below.

1 Installing the One-Click Wow! Presets. Inside the Adobe Photoshop Elements 2 folder installed on your computer, locate the Presets folder (**Adobe® Photoshop® Elements > Presets**).

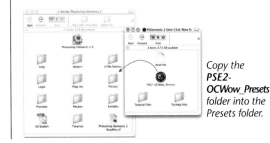

Finding the Presets folder

Insert the One-Click Wow! CD-ROM into your computer's CD-ROM drive **and double-click its icon** or use My Computer (Windows); locate and **copy the One-Click Wow! Presets folder into the Presets folder** that you found before.

Copy the PSE2-OCWow_Presets folder into the Presets folder.

2 Starting up the Adobe Photoshop Elements 2 program. To start up Elements 2, **double-click the Elements 2 icon** or in Windows **choose Start > Programs > Adobe > Photoshop Elements 2.**

Photoshop Elements 2.0

Double-click the Adobe Photoshop Elements 2 icon to start the program, or use the Start menu.

(If Elements is already running, you'll need to quit the program and start it again so it can "find" the **One-Click Wow! Presets** you've added to the Presets folder. To quit, choose **File > Exit** in Windows, or **File > Quit** on a Mac.)

For convenience in working with Styles, you'll need to have the Layers palette and Layer Styles palettes open. To open the Layers palette (if it is not already open), **choose Window > Layers, and then drag the palette's tab out of the docking area.** Open the Layer Styles palette the same way (**choose Window > Layer Styles and drag the palette out**).

So that you can see the full names of the Styles, click the **List View** button — the left button at the bottom of the palette.

The Layer Styles palette — open, out of the docking area, and in List View mode

3 Preparing the file. Now open the file that you want to "style" (**choose File > Open**). You can duplicate the file for safekeeping if you like; see the tip at the left.

Adobe Photoshop Elements

Styles can only be applied to layers. Do you want to make this background a layer?

Cancel   OK

Styles cannot be applied to a Background layer

So that you'll get good results right away when you apply a **One-Click Wow! Style** to the file, change the Resolution setting for the file as follows: **Choose Image > Resize > Image Size**; in the Image Size dialog box, **make sure the** "Resample Image" option is OFF (no check mark in the box). **Then double-click to select the number in the Resolution setting box and type in 225**; click OK to close the Image Size box.

Image Size

Pixel Dimensions: 9.01M

Width: 2100 pixels

Height: 1500 pixels

OK   Cancel   Help

Document Size:

Width: 9.333 inches

Height: 6.667 inches

Resolution: 225 pixels/inch

☑ Constrain Proportions

☐ Resample Image: Bicubic

Changing the Resolution setting to 225 pixels/inch

4 Applying the Style. To target the layer where you want to apply a **One-Click Wow! Style, click the layer's name in the Layers palette.** (You can't apply a Style to the *Background;* see the tip at the left.)

The layer is targeted and ready for a Style to be applied.

To apply one of the **One-Click Wow! Styles** to this layer, first click **the pop-up menu in the top left corner of the Layer Styles palette and choose the set of Styles you want.** (To get a good look at the contents of each set so you can decide which one you want to choose, look at the examples throughout this book.) Then click the particular Style you want to apply.

*Choosing the **WowPSE2-02 Frame Styles** set* *Applying the **Wow-Frame 03** Style*

The Style will be applied to your file instantly! In the Layers palette the *f* icon next to the layer name shows that a Style has been added.

*The **Wow-Frame 03** Style has added a textured frame and a beige mat to the photo.*

To find out about customizing Layer Styles and saving "styled" files, read on. Pages 8–17 provide pointers, and you'll find a tutorial on pages 18–21.

SAMPLES GALLERY

Here (and continued at the end of the chapter on pages 22–25) are just a few samples of what you can do with the twenty different libraries that make up the **One-Click Wow Styles.** As you can see, all the Layer Styles conform to whatever shape is on the particular layer that they are applied to — whether that is a photograph or a graphic. For some of the images shown here, the Styles have been scaled to fit the specific subject.

👁 *See "Scaling a Style" on page 9 for tips on scaling.*

1 *Frame 02, and* **6** *Frame 04, are wooden frames with mats.* **2** *Frame 08 is a woven frame that has been scaled here 200%.* **3** *Gems 13 turns type into a abalone shell sculpture under resin.* **4** *Like all styles,* **Halo 06**'s *grainy light and dark edges conform to the shape of the content of the layer.* **5** *Tint FX 04 is a sepiatone treatment with an inner glow and outer shadow.* **7** *Plastic 09 is a transparent blue/green color.* **8** *Metals 04 imitates hand beaten gold.* **9** *Edges 07 "coats" anything on the layer with glossy plastic.* **10** *Halo 08 is a rounded emboss.* **11** *Metals 01 is rusted and pitted, and* **12** *Frame 10 has a floral pattern and matching mat.*

continued on page 22

6

7

8

9

10

11

12

1

Using One-Click Wow! Styles

T he next 20 pages show how to work with the **One-Click Wow! Styles** to transform your Photoshop Elements 2 projects from "ho-hum" to "Wow!" instantly. Whether you start with type, graphics, photos, or Photoshop Elements 2 paintings like those shown in "Section 4" of this book, you can achieve professional results with just one click in the Styles palette.

You'll also learn how to scale a Style, if necessary, to fit your particular project. Any **Wow Style** can be used as a starting point for customizing Styles of your own, by changing one or more component effects and then saving the "Styled file" so you can copy and paste your Style to use elsewhere. A quick "Layer Style Tutorial" starting on page 18 will lead you step-by-step through applying, customizing, and saving Styled files.

To make sure you get the best-looking output possible, you'll find a section (pages 15–17) on how to prepare Photoshop Elements files for successful output, either in print or on the web.

▶ *One-Click Wow! Styles can be applied to files of any resolution, but they are easiest to work with in files whose Resolution setting is 225 pixels/ inch.* ◉ *See the tip on page 9 for more.*

WHAT IS A LAYER STYLE?

A Style is a way to improve photos, type, or graphics — instantly! — by "overlaying" color, texture, dimension, framing and a dozen other effects.

▶ *The Wow Presets on the **Adobe Photoshop Elements 2 One-Click Wow! CD-ROM** are provided as an indispensable companion to the Adobe Photoshop Elements program. But Presets can also be used with the full **Adobe Photoshop** program (version 6 or later). To take advantage of this, we created an edition of **One-Click Wow!** made just for Photoshop.*

Simply stated, a Layer Style is a "look" that you can add to photos, type, or graphics *instantly* — simply by clicking in the Layer Styles palette. Below are a few of the highly sophisticated kinds of effects you can apply with the Styles from the **One-Click Wow! CD-ROM.** To create such a treatment *without* using Layer Styles could take a lot of time, work, and skill, as shown at the right.

*A Style can be a color treatment such as a "partial sepiatone" (**Wow-Tint FX 01**) or an improvement to color and contrast (**Wow-Darkroom 04**).*

*A Style can provide edge effects for photos, such as a modern border treatment (**Wow-Edges 05**) or an antique wooden frame (**Wow-Frame 05**).*

*A Style can turn plain type or graphics into convincing material objects, such as chiseled steel (**Wow-Metals 17**) or transparent blue plastic (**Wow-Plastics 08**).*

At the Wow! intergalactic headquarters, we used the following "ingredients" to cook up the **One-Click Wow! Layer Styles:**

- A **drop shadow,** sharp or soft
- An **inner shadow** that extends inward from the edge of the artwork, which can produce a "carved" effect
- Light or dark **glows** that extend inward or outward from the edges of the art
- A **beveled edge,** wide or narrow, sharp or rounded
- An **overlay** of a single color, gradient, or pattern that changes or even replaces the original color of a photo, type, or graphic
- An **opacity** control that can make the original artwork partly or fully transparent
- A **texture** that creates bumps and pits on the surface of the artwork
- A **stroke** — even a multicolor stroke — that outlines the edges of the art
- A **"satin"** treatment that can add sophisticated reflection and refraction effects

To turn a solid gray circle into the gemstone lozenge above, you can apply the **Wow-Gems 02** Layer Style with just one click. Or you can try to construct the 11-layer file shown at the right. The choice is pretty much a "no-brainer!"

Bevel shadow

Bevel highlight

Inner shadow

Inner glow

"Satin" effect

Color overlay

Pattern overlay

Original gray circle

Outer glow

Drop shadow

Background

LAYER STYLE "MAGIC"

After you apply a Style, it's easy to make changes to the layer content or to the Style itself.

▶ To remove a Layer Style from a layer, you can click the **Clear Style icon** in the upper right of the Layer Styles palette, or "apply" the first Style in each of the One-Click Wow! Styles sets, as shown here:

▶ For a "hands-on" tutorial that leads you through the steps of scaling, customizing, copying, and pasting Styles, you can follow "A Layer Style Tutorial" on pages 18–21, using the Tutorial files on the CD-ROM.

---

ayer Styles are so flexible! Once you've applied a Style, **you can change the content of the layer and the Layer Style will conform to the changes.**

*If you apply a Style (here **Wow-Metals 06**) to a type layer and then change the font, the Style is retained.*

You can even edit the text, and the Style will conform to the new wording.

*If you reshape your graphics or clip art, the Style (here **Wow-Metals 19** with its beveled edge and highlighting) conforms to the new shape.*

*If you paint or draw on a layer that already has a Style applied to it, the Style (here **Wow-Plastic 07**) will automatically be added to each new stroke as you create it.*

---

ot only can you change the content of a "styled" layer (as shown in the examples at the left), but **you can also change the Style.** A Style change can mean that you **completely replace the Style:**

*Here the **Wow-Metals 06** Style (top) was removed (center) and **Wow-Chrome 10** was applied.*

Or instead of replacing it, you can **modify a Style** by scaling it, by changing one or more of its settings, or by applying another Style without removing the first, to combine characteristics of both Styles. The next six pages tell how to:

- **Scale a Style** that was designed for a bigger or smaller or fatter or thinner element so it's a "custom fit" for your own graphics or type (pages 9–10).
- **Customize a Style** to change its lighting or thickness characteristics (page 11).
- **Combine Styles** to apply the effects of more than one Style to the same layer (page 12).
- **Copy a Layer Style** so you can apply it to another layer, either in the same file or in a different one (page 13).
- **Use a Style with a clipping group** to mask an image and "style" it as well (page 14).

Scaling a Style

To "custom-fit" a Layer Style to a particular file, try scaling the Style.

▶ *All Layer Styles are originally created in the full version of Adobe Photoshop, and every file has its own Resolution setting. The **One-Click Wow! Styles** were created in files with a Resolution setting of 225 pixels/inch (since this is a good resolution to use when printing to both desktop printers as well as commercial printing presses). Although these Styles can be applied to files with any Resolution setting, they are easiest to work with if you first make sure the Resolution setting for your file is 225 pixels/inch. You can do this — without altering your image at all — by choosing **Image** > **Resize** > **Image Size**, then making sure* "Resample Image" is turned OFF, *and then typing in "225" for the Resolution setting, as explained in step 3 of the "One-Click Wow! Quick Start" on pages 2–3.*

After you apply a Layer Style, there's a good chance you'll want to scale it. That's because a Style can look different depending on whether you apply it to a thick or thin graphic, a bold or light-weight typeface, or a large or small photo.

1 Applying the Style. Apply a Layer Style as described in "One-Click Wow! Quick Start" on pages 2–3 or in "Copying a Layer Style" on page 13.

Great Grandma's portrait needs a frame.

*But the frame and mat applied by the **Wow-Frame 03** Style (page 25) seem to cover up too much of the image. The Style needs to be scaled.*

2 Scaling. Choose Layer > Layer Style > Scale Effects. Pop out the Scale slider by clicking the little triangle to the left of the "%" sign, and move the slider until the Layer Style looks right. Or type in a specific percentage, according to the suggestions in the *Note* below.

Scaling the Style to 50% improves the framing.

Note: There are some important options to consider when you apply a Layer Style that includes a pattern or texture effect:

• First, certain Scale percentages work best for keeping the surface markings or texture of a Layer Style sharp and clear. (The **One-Click Wow! Styles** that include pattern or texture have an **asterisk [*]** after their names in the Layer Styles palette and in the examples shown on pages 32–75 of this book.) If you've made sure that the Resolution setting of your file is 225 pixels/inch (as

▶ *It's possible to scale a Layer Style so small that some of its features go away — for instance, the bevel or drop shadow could disappear if you were to set a very low Scale value in the Scale Effects dialog box and then click OK to close the box. Once you've scaled a file too small, you may not be able to successfully scale it up again. If that happens, you can clear the Style from the Layer, then apply the Style again and scale again, this time not as small.*

described in the tip on page 9), these optimal percentages are 25%, 50%, 100% (no scaling), and 200%. If none of these percentages is ideal for your project, you may need to accept a somewhat soft-looking pattern in order to get the ideal width of the frame, for instance. (Styles that *don't* include a surface pattern or texture don't have an asterisk [*] in their names, and you don't have to worry about restricting the Scale setting to one of these values.)

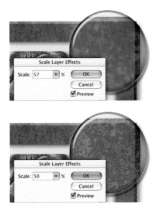

*Scaling the **Wow-Frame 03** Style to 57% blurs the pattern (top), but using a Scale factor of exactly 50% keeps the pattern sharp.*

• Second, when you reduce the Scale of a patterned or textured Style, **the repeat in the pattern may become more apparent.** For instance, if you look carefully at the frame around Great Grandma's portrait in step 2 on page 9, you can see that the repeating pattern that's used to create the texture is more obvious than it was in step 1, when the Style was first applied at the default 100% Scale setting. In this case we chose to allow the repeat to show in order to get the right width for the frame, since the repeat wasn't distracting.

If you apply one of the **One-Click Wow! Styles** to **a file whose Resolution is *not* set to 225 pixels/inch,** you may get a result that looks different from the sample shown in this book. Here are some examples of **Wow-Frame 03** applied to exactly the same file but with four different, commonly used Resolution settings:

72 pixels/inch   *150 pixels/inch*

225 pixels/inch   *300 pixels/inch*

If you apply a Wow Style to a file whose Resolution is *not* set at 225 pixels/inch, here are some settings you can use in the Scale Effects dialog box in order to help keep it sharp if it has a pattern. The percentages in bold type will produce the same results as the default 100% Scale in a 225 pixels/inch file. (Again, Styles without a surface pattern or texture don't have an asterisk [*] after the name, and you don't have to worry about these special Scale settings.)

72 pixels/inch: 78%, 156%, **312%**, 624%

150 pixels/inch: 75%, **150%**, 300%

300 pixels/inch: 75%, 150%, 300%

Customizing Style Settings

Photoshop Elements 2 lets you alter some of the component effects of a Style.

▶ *Besides changing the individual component effects, you can also scale all the effects in the Style together, as described in "**Scaling a Style**" on page 9.*

▶ *When you apply a Layer Style to a layer, the 🅕 icon appears to the right of the layer's name in the Layers palette. You can double-click this 🅕 to open the Style Settings dialog box.*

▶ *With the Style Settings dialog box open, you can change the Lighting Angle and the Shadow Distance simply by moving the cursor into your image and dragging — instead of using the sliders or typing numbers into the dialog box.*

The Style Settings dialog box lets you adjust some of the effects that make up a Layer Style. To open the Style Settings box, click on the layer's name in the Layers palette and then **choose Layer > Layer Style > Style Settings**. (If some characteristics are dimmed in the Style Settings box, it's because the current Style doesn't include those effects. For instance, if the Outer Glow Size slider is dimmed, it's because the Layer Style doesn't include an Outer Glow.) As you change the settings, you can compare "before" and "after" views by turning the "Preview" off and on.

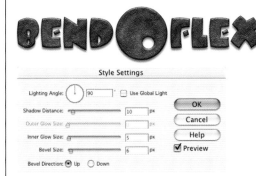

*If you apply the **Wow-Metals 07** Style and open the Style Settings dialog box, you can see the built-in settings for the Lighting Angle, Drop Shadow, Inner Glow, and Bevel.*

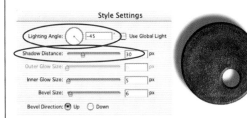

*Changing the **Lighting Angle** moves the shadow to the upper left and also shifts the highlights and shadows of the Bevel. Changing the **Shadow Distance** increases the shadow's offset, lifting the logo farther off the surface of the page.*

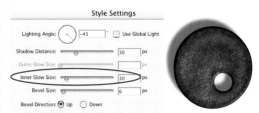

*The **Inner Glow** in the Metals 07 Style was designed to have a darkening effect inside the edge, rather than the lightening effect typically applied with a Glow. Increasing the Inner Glow Size to 30 pixels spreads the dark area farther inward.*

*Increasing the **Bevel Size** makes the "styled" type look thicker. Notice that for a Style like this one that has a surface texture built-in, **increasing the Bevel Size also increases the "bump" in the texture**, making the surface look rougher.*

You can find the **Bend-O-Flex** file on the **One-Click Wow!** CD-ROM and experiment with the Style Settings yourself.

Combining Styles

In Elements you can combine effects from two or more Styles by applying the Styles one after the other.

▶ *To remove a Layer Style from a layer, you can click the* **Clear Style icon** *in the upper right of the Layer Styles palette, or "apply" the first Style in each of the One-Click Wow! Styles sets (its icon looks like this:☐).*

▶ *When you arrive at a combination of Styles you like and you think you might want to use it again, the way to save the combined Style in Elements 2 is to save (in Photoshop format) a file you've applied it to. Whenever you want to use the combined Style again, open this file and copy and paste the Style as described in "Copying a Layer Style" on page 13.*

In Photoshop Elements 2, Layer Styles are cumulative. That means you can apply one Style and then change or add effects by applying another Style. (This is different than in the full version of Photoshop, where applying a new Style completely replaces the previous one.) **A newly added Style will change only those effects that are built into it**, leaving alone all the other effects of the preexisting Style.

To combine Styles, apply one as described in the **"One-Click Wow! Quick Start"** on pages 2–3, or by copying and pasting as described in "Copying a Layer Style" on page 13. Then apply another one. You can keep combining Styles until you arrive at a combination you like.

We applied the **Wow-Frame 07** Layer Style, which doesn't include a mat.

Then we applied the **Wow-Mat 01** Style, which added a mat but didn't affect the frame.

The white mat wasn't the perfect color, so we applied **Wow-Mat 03**. The new mat replaced the white one.

Finally, we decided we preferred it without the mat and simply removed it by clicking on **Wow-Mat 00-none.**

In some of the **One-Click Wow! Style** sets you'll find "extras" at the bottom of the listing in the Layer Styles palette. For instance, the **Wow-Frame** set includes a series of **Wow-Mat** Styles as well as the **Wow-Shadow** series that's also supplied with all of the other Wow-Styles sets.

The **Wow-Shadow** *Layer Styles that are included in all of the Wow-Styles sets includes a* **"None"** *option that will remove the drop shadow from an applied Style that has one.*

Another way that Styles can be "combined" is to layer "styled" elements: Apply one Style to the top layer and another Style to the layer underneath. An example of such an arrangement is shown below, and you'll find other examples on page 50.

To create the look of a carved translucent amulet, the **Wow-Gems 19** *Style was applied to a graphic on the upper layer, and the lighter* **Wow-Gems 08** *was applied to an oval shape on the layer below.*

Copying a Layer Style

Styles can be copied from layer to layer or even file to file.

▶ *The **One-Click Wow Test** file on the CD-ROM consists of five layers — a photo and four copies of the example graphic shown on pages 52–75 of this book. You can use this file as a "vault" for storing Layer Styles that you customize, and as a visual reference for what your customized Styles look like: Simply copy and paste your Style onto one of the layers of this file (as described at the right) and resave the file (File > Save). (As you need more layers for storing Styles, you can simply duplicate the photo or graphic layer by dragging its name to the "Create a new layer" button ⬚ at the bottom of the Layers palette.)*

*To use the stored Style again, open the **One-Click Wow Test** file, target the layer that has the Style you want, and copy and paste the Style.*

It's quick and easy to apply a preset Style by clicking its name in the Layer Styles palette, as described in "One-Click Wow! Quick Start" on pages 2–3. But if you modify that Style by scaling it, changing its settings, or combining it with other Styles, Elements 2 provides no way to save your new Style as a preset that will appear in the Layer Styles palette. There *is* an easy way to save a modified Style, though: Save the file it's applied to (in Photoshop format) and when you want to use it again, open the file and copy the Style, then paste it where you want to use it. Here's how to copy a Layer Style:

1 Target the layer that has the customized Layer Style already applied to it by clicking the layer's name in the Layers palette.

*The **Wow-Edges 05** Style had been applied to the "HT's On Fire" layer and then scaled to 30% (Layer > Layer Style > Scale Effects). This layer was targeted in the Layers palette.*

2 Choose Layer > Layer Style > Copy Layer Style.

Copying the customized Style

3 Target the layer where you want to apply the copied Layer Style, by clicking this layer's name in the Layers palette. (If you want to apply the Style to a different file, **open the file by choosing File > Open, and target the layer.**)

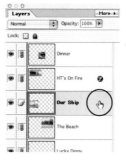

Clicking to target the "Our Ship" layer where we wanted to apply the copied Style

4 Choose Layer > Layer Style > Paste Layer Style.

Pasting the copied Style

5 Continue pasting by targeting a layer and **choosing Layer > Layer Style > Paste Layer Style**, until all the layers you want are "styled."

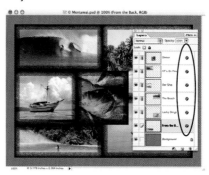

The copied Style was pasted to all the other photo layers. The shared Style helps unify the six assembled images.

Using Styles with Clipping Groups

A clipping group provides a way to mask an image inside a shape or type.

▶ *Any layer that can have transparency (any layer other than the Background) can have a Layer Style applied to it (here we used Wow-Glass 12), AND can be used as a cookie cutter to "clip" whatever layer is above it to its own shape, even a type layer.*

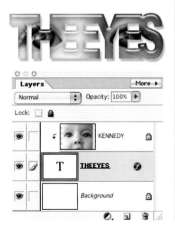

In Elements 2, a *clipping group* can be used to mask an image inside a graphic, a shape, or type: **Set the type or draw the shape on a layer below the image; then hold down the Alt key (Windows) or the Option key (Mac) and move the cursor onto the borderline between the two layers until it changes into an interlocking-circles icon, then click.** The lower layer will act like a "cookie cutter," limiting where the image in the upper layer is allowed to show.

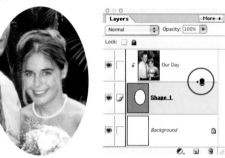

Alt- or Option-clicking on the borderline between layers will form a clipping group. The name of the "cookie cutter" (clipping) layer is underlined in the Layers palette, and the name of the clipped layer is indented.

If you choose the Move tool ⊹ and click in the Layers palette to target the clipped layer, you can drag the image around until the preferred image area shows in the clipping shape.

Dragging the "clipped" image repositions it inside the clipping shape.

If you add a Layer Style to the bottom ("clipping") layer of a clipping group, it affects the entire clipping group.

*The **Wow-Frame 04** Style (with its mat removed — see page 12 for more on Combining Styles), applied to the clipping layer, frames the clipped image.*

If you modify the clipping shape, as shown below, the Style conforms to the new shape.

After the original photo layer was recentered, the oval shape was enlarged (Image > Transform > Free Transform) to hold both people.

SAVING, SIZING & OUTPUT

For maximum flexibility, save in Photoshop format. Then choose the right size and format for output — whether printing directly from Elements 2 or saving a copy in a different format for placing your image in another program, attaching it to an email, or posting it on a Web page.

As you work on "styling" a file in Elements 2, it's a good idea to save the file periodically in the native Photoshop format. This will keep all the image information that you build into the file "alive" — including layers and Layer Styles — so you can go back and make changes to them later if you like.

Saving your layered file. The first time you save your file, **choose File > Save As.** In the Save As dialog box, **choose Photoshop** for the Format; make sure the "As a Copy" box is NOT checked and the "Layers" box IS checked, so the layers and Layer Styles will be preserved. Name the file, then click the **Save** button.

Save As:	Our Day.psd
Format:	Photoshop
Where:	Desktop
Save:	As a Copy / Layers
Color:	Embed Color Profile: Apple Cinema Display
File Extension:	Append / Use Lower Case

The Save As dialog box, set up for saving a layered file in the flexible Photoshop format

For subsequent saves as you work on the file, **choose File > Save.** The file will be resaved in Photoshop format.

When you've finished applying and customizing Layer Styles, it's easy to get your Elements file sized and ready to print on your desktop printer, or ready to place in a page layout or word-processing program. (If your goal is to prepare an image for emailing or posting on a Web page, go to "Resizing for email or the Web" on page 17.)

Checking the size of your file for printing. Whether you'll be printing directly from Elements or placing a file in another program and printing from there, you can use the Image Size dialog box to figure out whether you want to print the image "as is" or whether you'll want to reduce its dimensions before you print:

Choose Image > Resize > Image Size. Make sure the "Resample Image" box is NOT checked. (The tip at the top of page 16 tells why this is important.) If the size you want is different from the current Width and Height settings, type in the **Width** or **Height** value you want. When you change either of these dimensions, the other one will change automatically to keep the image in proportion, and the **Resolution** setting will change also.

If the new Resolution setting is *at least* as high as one of the following, your file has plenty of information for printing at the size you've entered. As a rule of thumb:

• **A safe Resolution setting for inkjet printing** or for a photo printer is **150 pixels/inch** or higher.

• **A safe Resolution setting for commercial printing on a press** is **225 pixels/inch** or higher.

The low Resolution value in the Image Size dialog box means that if this file were to be printed at 8 x 10 inches, the print would look "pixelated" (with visibly jagged edges).

SAVING, SIZING & OUTPUT

continued

▶ With *"Resample Image"* turned OFF in the Image Size dialog box, **none of the changes you make in the box will change any of the pixels** (the square dots that make up the image file). For example, if you **reduce the Width/Height dimensions,** you are telling Elements to keep each of the pixels exactly the same color it is, but print all the pixels smaller. That way each one will take up less space and they can be packed more tightly to make a smaller, sharper printed image.

On the other hand, if you **increase the dimensions,** again the pixels aren't changed, but they will be printed larger. You just need to be careful that pixel size doesn't get so large — in other words Resolution (pixels/inch) doesn't get so low — that the pixels themselves can be seen, usually as jagged edges in areas of contrast.

▶ With *"Resample Image"* turned ON in the Image Size dialog box, **changing dimensions actually changes the number of pixels in the file:** Elements "throws away" some pixels to make the image smaller. Or it "invents" the new pixels it needs for making the image bigger. Either of these processes can make the image look a bit "soft," or fuzzy, so sharpening may be required.

If your file's Resolution setting falls in one of the "safe" zones described on page 15, you can proceed to "Printing from Elements to your desktop printer" (below) or "Preparing a duplicate file to place in another program" (at the right).

Resizing the file for printing if you need to.

If your file's Resolution setting is less than the appropriate "safe" value on page 15, **you can print the image smaller** by reducing the Width/Height dimensions until the Resolution setting rises to a safe number.

Reducing the Width and Height to 5 x 4 inches raised the Resolution setting high enough so this file could be printed on a desktop inkjet printer.

By reducing the dimensions with "Resample Image" turned OFF, you are telling Elements to keep each pixel (square dot) in the image exactly the same color but make all the pixels print smaller so they can be packed tighter (more pixels/inch) on the printed page. With the pixels smaller, your eye won't be able to detect the individual square dots in the printed image.

Printing from Elements to your desktop printer.

Once your dimensions are set and your Resolution setting is safe, if you're printing directly from Photoshop Elements to your desktop printer, you're all set. All you have to do is **choose File > Print Preview**, and then make sure that your printer's options are set up to best match the paper

you're using. Some printers also have advanced options for improving the print quality of photos or artwork.

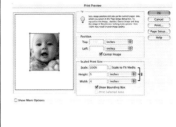

The Print Preview dialog allows you to check your image size settings, reposition the image on the page, or go to the Page Setup dialog where you can change paper size and orientation.

Preparing a duplicate file to place in another program. If your image will be placed and printed from within a word-processing or page layout program, you'll need to do just a little more work before you save the file. One good way to prepare a file for printing from another program is to save a flattened copy in **TIFF** format (*flattened* is Photoshop and Elements lingo for a file that consists only of a single *Background* layer).

First, to make a duplicate copy to flatten, **choose Image > Duplicate Image**.

Duplicating the file

Then, to flatten this copy, **choose Layer > Flatten Image**. This will make a single-*Background*-layer version of your file. It will show all the Style effects that you've built into the file, but the separate layers and Styles will no longer be available for changing. Transparency will be replaced with white, and any type will no longer be "live." That's why it was important to flatten a *copy* but also to save the original "live" file in Photoshop format (see page 15).

Now save this duplicate file by choosing **File > Save As** and selecting an appropriate format, such as **TIFF**, from the Format list in the Save As dialog box (the tip at the left tells about choosing file formats). Name the file, choose where you want to save it, and click the **Save** button.

If you're saving your duplicate file to display on the screen — for instance, as an attachment to email or on a Web page — you may want to reduce its pixel dimensions so the entire image will fit, even on a small screen.

Resizing for email or the Web. Open the Image Size dialog box (**Image > Resize > Image Size**). Turn "Resample Image" ON and also turn "Constrain Proportions" ON. In the **Pixel Dimensions** section at the top of the box, type in the appropriate number of pixels for **Width** or **Height.** If you haven't been told what pixel dimensions to use, limit the Width to no more than 580 pixels and the Height to no more than 400 pixels.

The "Resample Image" option must be turned ON in order to change the Pixel Dimensions.

Sharpening. Changing the dimensions of a file with "Resample Image" turned ON can cause the image to look slightly fuzzy. To bring back some of the original detail, you can use the **Unsharp Mask** filter: Either **choose Filter > Sharpen > Unsharp Mask,** or open the Filters palette (Window > Show Filters) and click the Unsharp Mask thumbnail

in the alphabetized listing, then click the Apply button. The Unsharp Mask filter looks for "edges" and accentuates the contrast between one side of the edge and the other. When the Unsharp Mask dialog box opens, experiment with the settings. You may want to start with Amount set at 50%, Radius at 1 pixel, and Threshold at 0 levels, and then increase the Amount if needed.

In the Unsharp Mask dialog box, ***Amount*** *controls how much the contrast is increased.* ***Radius*** *controls how many pixels in or out from the "edge" will have their contrast increased.* ***Threshold*** *controls how different the two sides of an "edge" have to be before the filter will sharpen it.*

Saving the file. Save the file (**File > Save As**) in **JPEG** format. Clicking the Save button opens the JPEG Options dialog box:

If your main goal is small file size, try starting with a setting of 3, with "Baseline Optimized" checked. Then work your way up to higher quality until you reach the biggest file size you're willing to accept. (Make sure "Preview" is turned on so you can watch the changes.)

Instead of using File > Save As, you can optimize the image (reduce the file size as small as possible without losing too much image quality) by using **File > Save For Web** (to learn about using Save For Web, choose Help > Photoshop Elements Help and choose "Optimizing Images for the Web and E-mail" from the list of topics).

► *As a rule of thumb, here are some formats that can be useful for saving in Elements:*

• *To keep all layers and Styles "alive" or to print an image to your desktop printer from within Elements, save in* ***Photoshop*** *(or .psd) format.*

• *If your goal is to place the image on a page in a page layout program,* ***TIFF*** *(.tif) works well in most cases.*

• *Because it can reduce file size so effectively,* ***JPEG*** *(.jpg) is a good format for posting on the Web or for attaching to an email. Note that JPEG compression can cause a noticeable reduction in image quality.*

• *If you want your file to be readable with Adobe Acrobat Reader (a free application that works on both Windows and Mac), save in* ***Photoshop PDF*** *(.pdf) format.*

To read more about formats for saving files, in Elements choose Help > Photoshop Elements Help and choose the "Saving Images" topic.

A LAYER STYLE TUTORIAL

This step-by-step tutorial walks you through a sample project using Layer Styles:

1 *Setting up Elements 2 to work with Layer Styles*

2 *Applying Styles*

3 *Customizing a Style*

4 *Copying and pasting a Style*

5 *Converting a Background to a non-Background layer so a Style can be applied*

6 *Replacing a Style*

7 *Scaling a Style*

8 *Changing layer content but keeping the Style*

1 Preparing the file. Make sure the Wow Presets are loaded into Adobe Photoshop Elements 2 (if you need help loading the Styles, see "One-Click Wow! Quick Start" on page 2).

Next **make sure the Layers palette is open** (if not, **choose Window > Layers**; if the tab for the palette is in the docking area at the right side of the Options bar at the top of the screen, drag it out so the palette will stay open as you work).

Also open the Layer Styles palette in the same way, **choosing Window > Layer Styles.** Click the **List View button** at the bottom of the Layer Styles palette so you can see the full names of the Styles.

In the Layer Styles palette the List View option is chosen by clicking the left icon at the bottom of the palette. List View shows a tiny thumbnail plus the full name of each Style. The pop-up menu in the upper left corner provides a list of available Style libraries.

Choose File > Open and in the Open dialog box choose the **"Wow Tutorial-Before"** file from the Wow CD-ROM. This file is a postcard design, made up of a "stack" of layers:

- a *Background* at the bottom
- two Type layers with plain black type
- six layers with a photo in each

For a better look at the "anatomy" of the file, **you can click in the "eye" column to temporarily turn off visibility for the *Background*,** so you can see the transparency that surrounds the type and the photos. (Photoshop Elements represents transparency as a checkerboard pattern so you can distinguish it from a solid white fill.)

None of the layers in this file has a Layer Style applied to it yet. But with each element on a layer of its own, you'll be able to add color and dimension by applying a different Style to each individual layer, as described next.

The "Wow Tutorial-Before" file, with visibility toggled off for the Background layer

2 Applying Layer Styles. Apply Layer Styles to the two type layers and the central photo layer as follows: For each layer, **click on its name** in the Layers palette to target the layer. Then apply a Style by choosing a set of Styles from the pop-up list in the upper-left corner of the Layer Styles palette and then clicking on the particular Style you want to apply. Try these Styles:

- For the **"Mentawai"** type layer, choose the **WowPSE2-15 Organics Styles set**, then click the **Wow-Organics 05** Style. This style adds a drop shadow, a dimensional edge, and a pattern fill to the type.

- For the **"a really cool place"** layer, choose the **WowPSE2-17-Stroke Styles set**, then choose the **Wow-Stroke 01** Style to add a drop shadow and a pattern fill (the pattern isn't very obvious in this small type — it just looks like variegated color).

> To toggle visibility on or off for any layer, click in the eye 👁 column, to the left of the layer's thumbnail in the Layers palette.

> A shortcut for opening the Style Settings dialog box so you can customize the Style on a layer is to **double-click the ƒ icon** for the layer in the Layers palette.

- For the layer with the center "**Dinner**" photo, choose the **WowPSE2-03 Tint FX Styles set**, then click the **Wow-Tint FX 01** Style, to add a sepiatone effect as well as a shadow and an inner glow around the edge.

Layer Styles applied to the two type layers and the "Dinner" photo layer. In the Layers palette, small "f" icons mark the "styled" layers.

3 Customizing a Style. Now you can customize one of the Styles you've applied. To reduce the width of the light border at the edge of the "Dinner" photo, **choose Layer > Layer Style > Style Settings** to open the Style Settings dialog box.

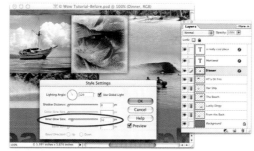

The built-in Size setting for the Inner Glow component of the Tint FX 01 Style is 32 px (pixels).

In the Style Settings box, **reduce the Inner Glow's Size setting** to 10 px (pixels). Then Click OK to close the box.

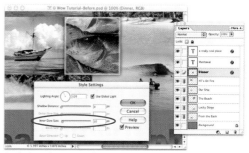

Reducing the Inner Glow Size setting shrinks the width of the light border.

4 Copying and pasting a Style. Now you can "style" all the other photos to match the customized Style on the "Dinner" layer by copying the Style from this layer and pasting it to the other layers, as follows: With the "**Dinner**" layer targeted in the Layers palette, **choose Layer > Layer Style > Copy Layer Style.**

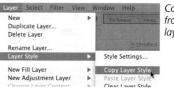

Copying the Style from the "Dinner" layer

Then target the "**HT's On Fire**" layer — one of the not-yet-styled layers — and apply the copied Style to it by **choosing Layer > Layer Style > Paste Layer Style.**

Pasting a Style to a targeted layer

The file after the copied Style is pasted to the "HT's On Fire" layer

Repeat this targeting-and-pasting process for each of the other four photo layers.

The file after the copied Style has been pasted to all the other photo layers

5 Converting a *Background*. You can use a **Wow-Style** to fill an entire layer with a pattern that consists of an image or texture. This can be a quick and easy way to make a background. For the "**Wow-Tutorial**" file you're working on, you can replace the gray fill in the background with a bamboo pattern. To do this target the *Background* in the Layers palette, then choose the **WowPSE2-15-Organics Styles set** of Layer Styles and then the **Wow-Organics 16** Style. An Alert Box will appear reminding you that "Styles can only be applied to layers. Do you want to make this background a layer?" To convert the *Background* to a layer that can have transparency

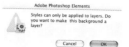

Converting the Background

(and thus can have a Layer Style) simply click OK; then in the New Layer dialog that appears, give the layer a name and click OK, and your style will be there.

*The file after the **Wow-Organics 16** Style has been applied to the bottom layer (The "**Wow Tutorial-During**" file shows the project at this stage.)*

6 Replacing Styles. You can change the entire "look and feel" of a Photoshop Elements composition simply by replacing some of Layer Styles, as follows: **Target the layer whose Style you want to change by clicking its name in the Layers palette.** Then choose **Layer > Layer Style > Clear Layer Style.** Then in the Layer Styles palette, **click the Style you want to apply.**

*The old Styles have been removed from the "Mentawai" type and the "Base Layer" and new ones (**Wow-Metals 06** and **Wow-Rock 20**, respectively) have been applied.*

▶ *If you try to apply a Style to a Background layer, an Alert Box will appear reminding you that "Styles can only be applied to layers. Do you want to make this background a layer?" To convert the background to a layer that can have transparency (and thus can have a layer style) simply click OK; then in the New Layer dialog that appears, give the layer a name and click OK, and your style will be there.*

► *To remove a Layer Style from a layer, you can click the **Clear Style icon** in the upper right of the Layer Styles palette, or "apply" the first Style in each of the **One-Click Wow! Styles** sets.*

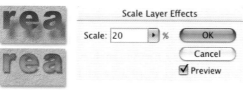

7 Scaling a Style. Scaling often helps to "custom-fit" a Style to a specific graphic. **Target the "a really cool place" layer** by clicking its name in the Layers palette. Then **choose Layer > Layer Style > Scale Effects.**

Choosing Scale Effects

In the Scale Layer Effects dialog box, click the little triangle to the right of the "100" to pop out the slider. Then **move the slider to the left** to reduce the pattern and the offset of the drop shadow. Moving the shadow makes the lettering seem closer to the background.

Before (top) and after reducing the Scale to 20%

The file after scaling the Style

8 Changing layer content. To demonstrate that **you can change the content of a layer without losing the Style**, try changing the font in the "Mentawai" layer: **Choose the Horizontal Type tool** T, in the Toolbox and

target the "Mentawai" layer in the Layers palette. Then choose a new font from the pop-up list in the Options bar at the top of the screen.

Before (left) and after changing the font (If you don't have the CCDutchCourage font, use a font of your choice.)

You can even change the wording in a "styled" Type layer: **Target "a really cool place"** in the Layers palette. In the main image window **drag the Type tool over the type** to select it.

The selected type

Next press the Caps Lock key on the left side of your keyboard and **type "BEYOND THE DREAM"** to change the wording. Click the check mark at the right end of the Options bar (or press **Enter**) to finalize the type change. Notice that the name of the layer changes in the Layers palette to reflect your editing.

After editing the type

To complete the tutorial, **change the font** for the "BEYOND THE DREAM" layer.

The "Wow Tutorial-After" file shows the project at this stage using the Dutch Courage font (available from www.comicbookfonts.com).

► *If your system doesn't have the same fonts as the system that originally created a particular file, you may get the following (or similar) alert. For these tutorials just click **Update**, then choose other fonts from the ones available on your computer.*

SAMPLES GALLERY

continued

1 An overlaid canvas texture is added to **Tint FX 09**'s brown duotone effect and inner glow and drop shadow. **2** **Stroke 09** has a grainy burgundy inner glow, a mustard-colored outer stroke and a hard-edged drop shadow. **3** **Chrome 02** is brightly lit with subtle reflections. **4** **Halo 01** has intense white and black inner and outer halos, as well as edging effects. **5** **Tint FX 09** applies a brown tint but keeps some of the original color. **6** **Darkroom 14** subtly lightens the center of a photo while darkening the edges (try **Darkroom 01, 03,** and **11–15** for similar subtle enhancements). **7** **Texture 02** adds a canvas texture overlay to any image or digital painting. **8** **Darkroom 07** "posterizes" a photo, with results based on the image's colors (try **Color FX 07** for a similar effect). **9** **Metals 19** is a chiseled polished steel which works great for graphics or type with lots of complex detail. **10** **Edges 01** adds a dark inner halo to a photo, while **12** **Edges 03** adds a bright halo. **11** **Glass 03** is a "chipped" polished glass effect. **13** **Organics 05** adds a dimensional stroke and a woven mat interior to text or graphics.

continued on page 24

SAMPLES GALLERY
continued

1 *Organics 11* is a recycled paper fill with beveled edges. **2** *Chrome 06* adds a dark, reflective dimensionality. **3** *Frame 05* is a hardwood (the Style has been scaled here 200% to better fit the photo. See page 9 for more on Scaling Styles). **4** *Stroke 15* adds a bright red fill, a brown stroke and a dark halo (also scaled here to better fit the graphic). **5** *Darkroom 08* adds drama to clouds and sunsets by overlaying a multicolored gradient (especially good for when the horizon is in the lower third of the photo). **6** *Stroke 11*'s grainy purple inner glow and golden stroke also works great with black on transparent clip art. **7** *Edges 09* inverts the color of an image at the edges. **8** *Tint FX 01*'s partial sepia overlay can give a quick hand-tinted effect. **9** *Stroke 03* is a simple white fill and black stroke and shadow. **10** *Organics 13*'s fill is a multicolored rust. **11** *Rock 18* turns anything into polished, chiselled granite, while **12** *Halo 12* is perfect for turning your logo into a subtle "watermark." **13** *Metals 16* is glowing antique gold. **14** *Frame 09*'s glass edges follow the contour of any piece of clip art. **15** *Tint FX 07* adds a blue color overlay with halos and **16** *Gems 07* instantly turns a piece of type or graphic into a granite counter top.

Southwestern Style

7

8

9

10

11

12

13

14

15

16

25

2 Styles for Photos

In this section you'll find **One-Click Wow! Styles** designed especially to enhance photos. Some of these Styles are also ideal for paintings you create using the methods described in Section 4.

▶ *It's likely that many of the photo files that you'll want to apply a Style to will need one of the changes below:*

- *If the image is a "flattened" file — that is, it consists only of a Photoshop "Background" — you'll want to double-click on its name to change it to a Layer so it can accept a Style*

Adobe Photoshop Elements

Styles can only be applied to layers. Do you want to make this background a layer?

Cancel   OK

- *Many of the **Wow Styles** for photos create edge treatments, such as dimensional frames. Some of the effects that are built into these Styles — for instance, Drop Shadows — are designed to extend outward from the edges of the image. For these effects to show up, you'll need extra space around the edges. To add space, choose Image > Resize> Canvas Size and increase the Width and Height.*

- *Many digital photos and scanned images are stored in the compressed JPEG format. Opening and then resaving these files as JPEGs again can create an obvious reduction in photo quality. So after you edit a JPEG — by applying a Style or any other way — be sure to save it in a different (lossless) format such as the native Photoshop (.psd) format.*

PHOTO GALLERY

On these next five pages are just a few samples of what you can do with the seven libraries of **Wow Styles designed specifically for applying to photographs.** (Pages 32–45 show examples of all of the Styles in these libraries.)

For some of the images shown here, the Styles have been scaled to fit. 👁 *See "Scaling a Style" on page 9 for tips on scaling.*

1 *Tint FX 06 turns a photo into a blue-tinted black & white, and adds a "pebble board" texture overlay as well.* **2 Color FX 10** *add a blue to green gradient overlay to a photo.* **3** *Edges 10's inner-edge treatment lightens, then inverts the photos's colors, creating a slightly different effect for each image.* **4** *Darkroom 06 turns the photo into a negative, while* **5** *Darkroom 10 combines both a red color overlay and a purple to yellow gradient for an intense recoloring (also good for enhancing sunset photos).*

continued on page 28

27

PHOTO GALLERY
continued

1 *Color FX 07* "colorizes" the photo, with the colors depending on the image. **2** *Edges 01* creates a vignette for use on a white background. **3** *Frame 04* is used here with its mat color changed, as described on page 34. **4** *Edges 08's* negative edges conform to the content of the photo. **5** *Tint FX 03* is a "75% sepiatone;" it applies a brown tint but keeps some of the original color (compare examples 18 and 19 on page 31). **6** *Framing several photos with the same Style (here Frame 07)* helps unify them as a group. **7** *Darkroom 09* adds drama to clouds and sunsets by overlaying a red-to-yellow gradient. **8** Used on this color photo, *Edges 08* inverts the color to form a custom edge. **9** *Tint FX 06* creates a textured blue duotone effect with a soft inner edge and outer shadow.

continued on page 30

1

2

3

4

5

6

7

8

9

10

PHOTO GALLERY
continued

10 Here ***Darkroom 04***'s exaggerated color makes a lively image even more so. **11** ***Edges 03***'s soft, dark edges, combined with the round-cornered framing, enhance the antique character of this photo. **12** ***Frame 05***'s dark beveled wood also adds to the antique look of this photo. **13** The lightly etched border of ***Frame 09*** lends the modern look of a slip-in glass frame. **14** ***Frame 06*** creates the "retro" look of tortoiseshell Bakelite. **15** ***Texture 04*** overlays a canvas-and-brush-stroke pattern. **16** The dark semitransparent border in ***Edges 05*** provides a modern framing treatment. **17** Here ***Darkroom 04*** builds color (compare the exaggerated effect in 10).

18 ***Tint FX 01*** overlays a 60% sepiatone on the original color and adds both a glow and a shadow to the edges. **19** ***Tint FX 09***'s sepia completely replaces the original color and also adds a canvas texture. **20** ***Edges 07*** puts the photo under clear, polished acrylic. **21** The stippled transparent borders of ***Edges 04*** allow whatever is on the layers below to show through. **22** ***Frame 03***'s beveled molding comes with a beige mat inside the frame. (Other mats, provided in the ***WowPSE2-02 Frame Styles*** set, can be "mixed and matched" with the dimensional frames (see "Combining Styles" on page 12.)

16

17

18

19

20

21

22

PHOTO EFFECTS SAMPLES

Edges

The **Wow-Edges** Layer Styles create vignettes and border treatments for photos. **Edges 06–10** include drop shadows. 👁 *See the tips on page 34 to learn how to convert a Background so you can apply a Style, and how to add space so the drop shadow can show.*

Edges 01 creates a soft-edged vignette for a photo that will be placed on a white background. **Edges 02** desaturates and lightens the edges. **Edges 03** darkens the border. **Edges 04** dithers to transparency, so it creates a "speckled vignette" that lets the background show through regardless of its color.

Edges 05 and **06** provide two speckled framing treatments.

The highlights at the edges of **07** create the look of an image under acrylic resin. This Style can be useful as a button treatment for a photo or an icon.

In **08–10** the shape and colors of the border area will vary, depending on the photo you apply it to, because these Styles invert the colors at the edges of the image. If you remove the drop shadow for **10,** it provides another "vignette to white" option.

ORIGINAL PHOTO: © CORBIS IMAGES ROYALTY FREE, COUPLES

Wow-Edges 01

Wow-Edges 02

Wow-Edges 03

Wow-Edges 04

Wow-Edges 05

Wow-Edges 06

Wow-Edges 07

Wow-Edges 08

Wow-Edges 09

Wow-Edges 10

Frames

With one click, each of the **Wow-Frame** Layer Styles creates a dimensional picture-frame treatment.

▶ *If you try to apply a Style to a Background layer, an Alert Box will appear reminding you that "Styles can only be applied to layers. Do you want to make this background a layer?" To convert the background to a layer that can have transparency (and thus can have a layer style) simply click OK; then in the New Layer dialog that appears, give the layer a name and click OK, and your style will be there.*

If you want to include the drop shadow that's built into these **Wow-Frame** Styles, there has to be some empty, transparent space around the image for the shadow to extend into.

▶ *To add empty space at the edges, choose Image > Resize> Canvas Size and increase the Width and Height.*

The **Wow-Frame** set also includes 10 **Wow-Mat** Styles to add different colored mats (as on **Frames 01–04**) to any of the frames. You can also change the drop shadow (even eliminate the shadow altogether) by adding one of the **Wow-Shadow** Styles in the **Wow-Frame** set.

Frames 01–05 are wood, **Frame 06** is tortoise shell and **Frame 07** and **08** are made of woven materials. **Frame 09** sandwiches an image between sheets of glass. 👁 *See the "Photo Gallery" on pages 28–31 for more description of individual **Wow-Frame** Styles and page 12 for more on "Combining Styles."*

ORIGINAL PHOTO: © JHDAVIS DESIGN

Wow-Frame 01*

Wow-Frame 02*

Wow-Frame 03*　　　　**Wow-Frame 04***

All of the **Wow-Frame Styles include surface patterns or textures. If you need to scale one of these Styles to fit your file, there are certain scaling percentages that will ensure that the patterns stay sharp and clear.* 👁 *See "Scaling a Style" on page 9 for help.*

Wow-Frame 05*

Wow-Frame 06*

Wow-Frame 07*

Wow-Frame 08*

Wow-Frame 09*

Wow-Frame 10*

Tints & Antique Effects

The **Wow-Tint FX** Styles create sepia-tone (**01–04**), black-and-white (**05**), blue tint (**06** and **07**) and antique effects (**08–10**), keeping different amounts of the original color. (Styles **02**, **05**, **08**, and **09** replace the original color entirely.)

All the **Wow-Tint FX** Styles except **05** include drop shadows. 👁 *See "Frames" on page 34 to learn how to add space so the drop shadow will show up.*

You can use any of the **Tint FX** series *without* the lightened or darkened edges. First apply the Style, then double-click the ℱ to the right of the layer's name in the Layers palette, click "Inner Glow Size" in the list of effects in the Style Settings dialog box, and in the Inner Glow section move the Size slider left to 0.

Tint FX 08 "antiques" an image by adding a dark edge, a slightly tinted black-and-white tone, and a "pebbled" surface. **Tint FX 09** is similar, but with a light edge and a canvas texture, and **10** has a subtler edge and a 5% contribution of the original color of the image.

ORIGINAL PHOTO: © JHDAVIS DESIGN

Wow-Tint FX 01

Wow-Tint FX 02

Wow-Tint FX 03

Wow-Tint FX 04

Wow-Tint FX 05

Wow-Tint FX 06*

Wow-Tint FX 07

Wow-Tint FX 08*

Wow-Tint FX 09*

Wow-Tint FX 10*

*Some of the **Wow-Tint FX** Styles include patterns or textures. If you need to scale one of these Styles to fit your file, there are certain scaling percentages that will ensure that the patterns stay sharp and clear. 👁 See "Scaling a Style" on page 9 for help.

Color Overlay Effects

The **Wow-Color FX** Styles use overlays of color — either solid colors or gradients — to create multicolor tints, changing the color of an image for practical or surreal and dramatic effects.

Styles **01** and **02** darken and lighten the image, respectively, so that the image can serve as a subtle background for light or dark type set in a layer above it.

Styles **03–07** create posterization and color-inversion special effects based on the colors in the original image.

The gradient overlays in **08–10** replace the color in the original image with multiple hues.

ORIGINAL PHOTO: © JHDAVIS DESIGN

ORIGINAL PHOTO: © CORBIS IMAGES ROYALTY FREE, FOOD PERSPECTIVES

Wow-Color FX 01

Wow-Color FX 02

Wow-Color FX 03

Wow-Color FX 04

Wow-Color FX 05

Wow-Color FX 06

Wow-Color FX 07

Wow-Color FX 08

Wow-Color FX 09

Wow-Color FX 10

Darkroom & Image-Enhancing Effects

Wow-Darkroom Styles **01–03** focus attention and add subtle enhancements; **01** darkens the top and bottom, **02** darkens the top only, and **03** darkens the edges and lightens the center.*

Style **04** exaggerates the saturation (or intensity) of the colors. (It will have no effect on a black-and-white picture.)

Style **05** adds a dark edging and also *solarizes* the image, turning some colors negative and leaving others positive. To use the effect without the darkened edges, you can apply the Style, then double-click the ⦿ icon in the Layers palette, and in the Style Settings dialog move the Inner Glow's Size slider to 0.

Style **06** makes a negative. And **07** converts the image to a limited range of colors; light colors turn yellow and orange, darker colors become gray.

Styles **08–10** are particularly good for enhancing sunset skies.

Wow-Darkroom 01

Wow-Darkroom 02

Wow-Darkroom 03

Wow-Darkroom 04

*Wow-Darkroom 11–15 are subtle variations on Wow-Darkroom 03.

Wow-Darkroom 05

Wow-Darkroom 06

Wow-Darkroom 07

Wow-Darkroom 08

Wow-Darkroom 09

Wow-Darkroom 10

Film Grain, Noise & Mezzotints

A pattern or texture can provide a subtle artistic treatment for a single image, or it can help to unify several photos.

Some of the Styles in the **Wow-Grain** set produce mezzotint-like effects, adding dots, lines, or streaks. Others (**01**–**03**) can simulate film grain or "digital noise." These can help hide pixel artifacts that may appear in low-resolution images or help unify photos in different layers of a collage.

Styles **04**–**06** are variations on a reticulated mezzotint effect, and **07** and **08** create irregular blotches for a freckled or dappled look.

Style **09** creates a diagonal pattern of brushed lines. And **10** creates a horizontal pattern of high-tech scan lines.

ORIGINAL PHOTO: © CORBIS IMAGES ROYALTY FREE, FOOD PERSPECTIVES

Wow-Grain 01*

Wow-Grain 02*

Wow-Grain 03*

Wow-Grain 04*

* *The names of all Styles in the* **Wow-Grain** *library include the * symbol, which indicates that a surface pattern or texture is part of the Style. If you need to scale one of these Styles to fit your file, there are certain scaling percentages that will ensure that the patterns stay sharp and clear.*
👁 See "Scaling a Style" on page 9 for help.

Wow-Grain 05*

Wow-Grain 06*

Wow-Grain 07*

Wow-Grain 08*

Wow-Grain 09*

Wow-Grain 10*

Paper, Canvas & Other Texture Overlays

When you create a painting in Photoshop Elements — whether "from scratch" or from a photo — adding the texture of paper or canvas can complete the illusion. The **WowPSE2-07 Texture Styles** can also simply be applied to a photo or graphic to add personality.

Wow-Texture 01 simulates watercolor paper. Style **02** is an irregularly textured canvas, **03** "bevels" any semi-transparent brush strokes you apply and adds a canvas texture as well, and **04** simulates canvas with impasto brush strokes. Style **05** simulates pebble board, **06** and **07** are rough surfaces for pastel or chalk, **08** is cracked paint, **09** simulates watercolor with salt stains, and **10** simulates the fresco effect of painting on a plastered surface.

The "painting" used in this example (a detail of which is shown below) was made from a photo by using Tool Presets from the **Wow Media Brushes** library.  *See "How to Paint with the Wow! Media Brush Presets" starting on page 79 to learn how to use the **Wow-Textures** in combination with the Wow Media Brush Presets.*

ORIGINAL PHOTO/PAINTING
© JHDAVIS DESIGN

Wow-Texture 01*

Wow-Texture 02*

Wow-Texture 03*

Wow-Texture 04*

** All of the **Wow-Texture** Styles include surface patterns or textures. If you need to scale one of these Styles to fit your file, there are certain scaling percentages that will ensure that the patterns stay sharp and clear. "Scaling a Style" on page 9 tells how.*

Wow-Texture 05*

Wow-Texture 06*

Wow-Texture 07*

Wow-Texture 08*

Wow-Texture 09*

Wow-Texture 10*

3

Styles for Type & Graphics

The Styles in this section (from **Wow** libraries **08–20**) were designed to add color, dimension, and material characteristics to type and graphics. Choose a Style for your project, apply it, and then tweak it if you like, as described on pages 9–14.

▶ *You can "combine" Styles by applying separate Styles to the layered elements of a graphic. For instance, to create the look of a carved, translucent amulet, the* **Wow-Gems 19** *Style was applied to a graphic on the upper layer, and the lighter* **Wow-Gems 08** *was applied to an oval shape on the layer below.*

◉ *For other examples of "combined" Styles, see page 50.*

TYPE & GRAPHICS GALLERY

The next five pages show some of the "magic" you can work on graphics and type using the 12 sets of Wow Styles on pages 52–75. (Some Styles have been scaled to fit the graphics shown here.)

1, 2, 3 *Rocks 03, 04,* and *05 are three different color versions of the same rough rock.*
4 *Rocks 12 is white stone.*
5 *The thick gold stroke of* **Stroke 09,** *which extends outward from all the edges of this black graphic, fills in the small negative spaces, leaving transparency only in the large sun element at the bottom.* **6** ***Chrome 17*** *applies a dark finish with bright, raised bevels at the edges.* **7** *After* **Plastic 19** *was applied, the rainbow Gradient Overlay was repositioned to put its colors where we wanted them.* **8** *The* **Rocks 02** *Style was scaled to 25% after it was applied.*
9 *Glass 19 makes the flat shapes and lettering of this type look like water.* **10** *Like many of the other Wow Styles designed for photos,* **Edges 05** *can work well on graphics also.*

continued on page 48

TYPE & GRAPHICS GALLERY

continued

11 Woods 06 *adds dimension and the grain and glow of smooth polished wood.*
12 Halo 13 *lightens the interior, adding an overall speckle and a dark outer "halo"; like most Styles with interior edge effects, it looks different on bolder elements than on thin ones.* **13 Metals 19** *simulates chiseled steel.* **14 Glow 03** *and **04** turn edges into glowing neon tubes.* **15 Stroke 06** *and **07** add color strokes and fills; sharp shadows add dimension.*
16 Rocks 01 *creates bricks, complete with indented mortar.* **17 Gems 19** *on the graphics and the lighter **Gems 08** on the oval in the layer below combine for a backlit effect.* **18 Plastic 15** *creates an opaque, polished surface.*
19 Metals 15 *adds the look of rusted, deeply pitted metal.*
20 Plastic 09 *produces a rounded, translucent blue-green.* **21 Stroke 20** *is great for "comic book" type.* **22** *In the **Chrome** set, **15** is darkest.*
23 Glass 20 *produces rounded smoked glass.* **24 Organics 19** *produces a rustic woven look.* **25 Halo 09** *"carves" into the surface of the layers below.*

continued on page 50

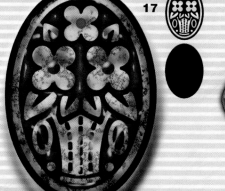

17

18

19

TOXIC

20

BEND O FLEX

22

JUST GOT
The Best
BETTER

21 *"Gee whiz!"*

23

24

 25

TYPE & GRAPHICS GALLERY
continued

26 **Glow 10** *turns the lines of this logo into neon tubes in the "off" state.* **27** **Glow 08** *turns the neon "on."* **28** **Stroke 14** *provides black and white outlines and a special gradient fill.* **29** **Plastic 05** *creates swirled color inside chrome edges.* **30** **Woods 18** *produces beveled pine.* **31** *Gradient-filled* **Stroke 18** *applied to a rectangle makes a surface for* **Halo 11**, *applied to a graphic in the layer above, to "carve" into.* **32** **Plastic 13** *applied to a layer above a shape treated with* **Plastic 14** *creates a stamped sign.* **33** *The bright placer gold of* **Metals 16** *on the star complements the duller bronze of* **Metals 15** *on the type.* **34** **Metals 09** *produces brushed steel with polished edges.* **35** **Halo 16** *adds a rainbow halo without changing the graphic's original color, here red.* **36** **Organics 04** *makes a raised green edge around a woven fill.* **37** **Halo 18** *makes the art disappear, leaving only a dark exterior halo.* **38** **Gems 11** *produces a raised abalone texture.* **39** **Chrome 13** *adds a matte finish to broad, flat areas.* **40** **Plastic 08** *is a clear, rounded blue.* **41** *The boldness of each part of the graphic determines how much of* **Glow 16**'s *yellow inner glow can color the interior.*

34

35

36

37

38

39

40

PLAY

41

GRAPHICS & TYPE EFFECTS SAMPLES

Chromes

The Layer Styles in the **Wow-Chrome** set were designed for use on type or graphics, to simulate various kinds of reflective surfaces. The Styles are shown here applied to a file with a Resolution setting of 225 pixels/inch.

Wow-Chrome 11 is the only one of these Layer Styles that allows some of the original color of the graphic or type to come through in the chrome. So if you had started with a green symbol, for instance, instead of the gray shown here, your chrome would show a slight green tint. All other **Wow-Chrome** Styles produce the same results regardless of the starting color.

*In Styles whose names include the * symbol, a built-in surface pattern or texture is used to create the illusion of the environment reflected in the chrome. If you need to scale one of these Styles to fit your file, there are certain scaling percentages that will ensure that the patterns stay sharp and clear.*

Original Graphic

Wow-Chrome 01*

Wow-Chrome 02*

Wow-Chrome 03

Wow-Chrome 04

Wow-Chrome 05

Wow-Chrome 06

Wow-Chrome 07

Wow-Chrome 08

Wow-Chrome 09

Wow-Chrome 10*

Wow-Chrome 11*

Wow-Chrome 12*

Wow-Chrome 13

Wow-Chrome 14*

Wow-Chrome 15

Wow-Chrome 16*

Wow-Chrome 17*

Wow-Chrome 18

Wow-Chrome 19

Wow-Chrome 20

Metals

The Layer Styles in the **Wow-Metals** set were designed to make type or graphics look like they were stamped, chiseled, molded, or otherwise created from gold, steel, iron, or other metals, some glowing hot. Rough-surfaced Styles typically use the same pattern both in a Pattern Overlay effect and in the Texture aspect of the Bevel And Emboss effect. The results shown here were achieved by applying each of the Styles to a file with a Resolution setting of 225 pixels/inch.

👁 *See "Scaling a Style" on page 9 for directions on adjusting Styles to fit specific graphics.*

* Styles whose names include the * symbol have a built-in surface pattern or texture. If you need to scale one of these Styles to fit your file, there are certain scaling percentages that will ensure that the patterns stay sharp and clear.
👁 *See "Scaling a Style," page 9.*

Original Graphic

Wow-Metals 01*

Wow-Metals 02*

Wow-Metals 03*

Wow-Metals 04*

Wow-Metals 05*

Wow-Metals 06*

Wow-Metals 07*

Wow-Metals 08*

Wow-Metals 09*   **Wow-Metals 10***   **Wow-Metals 11***   **Wow-Metals 12***

Wow-Metals 13*   **Wow-Metals 14***   **Wow-Metals 15***   **Wow-Metals 16***

Wow-Metals 17   **Wow-Metals 18**   **Wow-Metals 19***   **Wow-Metals 20**

Glass, Ice & Crystal

The Layer Styles in the **Wow-Glass** set were designed to make type or graphics look as if they were formed of transparent crystalline materials. Some of them also feature highly reflective textured surfaces.

The **Wow-Glass** Styles completely remove or replace the original color of the graphic, so that no matter what color it was to start with, the original color is not evident in the "styled" element.

The effects shown here are the results of applying the **Wow-Glass** Styles to a file with a Resolution setting of 225 pixels/inch. 👁 *See "Scaling a Style" on page 9 to learn about the relationship between Layer Styles and the Resolution setting.*

**Styles whose names include the * symbol have a built-in surface pattern or texture. If you need to scale one of these Styles to fit your file, there are certain scaling percentages that will ensure that the patterns stay sharp and clear. 👁 See "Scaling a Style," page 9.*

Original Graphic   **Wow-Glass 01**   **Wow-Glass 02**

Wow-Glass 03*   **Wow-Glass 04**   **Wow-Glass 05***

Wow-Glass 06   **Wow-Glass 07**   **Wow-Glass 08**

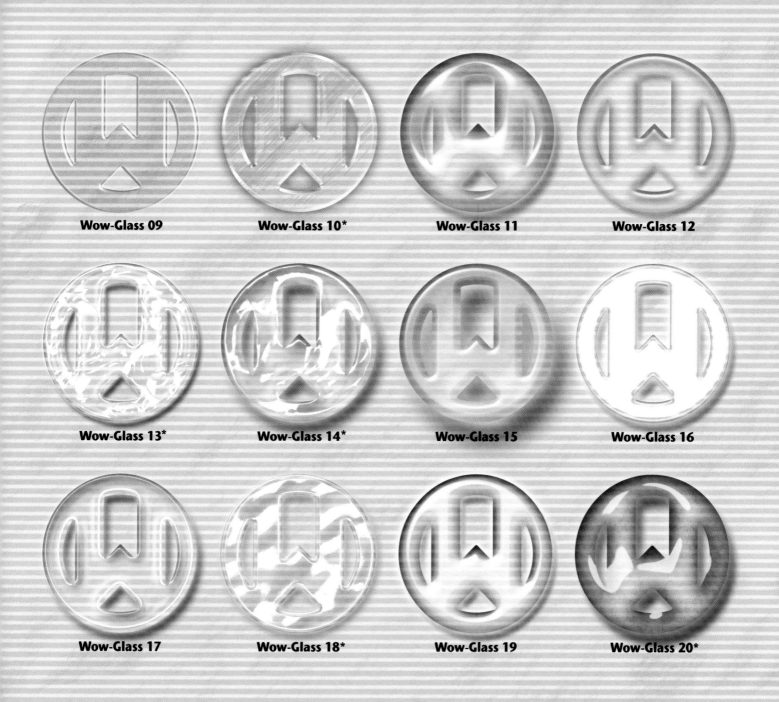

Wow-Glass 09

Wow-Glass 10*

Wow-Glass 11

Wow-Glass 12

Wow-Glass 13*

Wow-Glass 14*

Wow-Glass 15

Wow-Glass 16

Wow-Glass 17

Wow-Glass 18*

Wow-Glass 19

Wow-Glass 20*

Gems & Smooth Stones

The Layer Styles in the **Wow-Gems** set were designed to endow type or graphics with the colorful brilliance of polished gems, amber, or shells, as well as marble and other kinds of stone, with accompanying translucency and reflectivity.

All of the **Wow-Gems** Styles apply surface patterning, and one (**Wow-Gems 11**) has a bumpy surface texture as well.

The effects shown here are the results of applying the **Wow-Gems** Styles to a file with a Resolution setting of 225 pixels/inch. 👁 *See "Scaling a Style" on page 9 for the relationship between Layer Styles and the Resolution setting.*

*The names of all the Styles in the **Wow-Gems** set include the * symbol, which indicates that a surface pattern or texture is part of the Style. If you need to scale one of these Styles to fit your file, there are certain scaling percentages that will ensure that the patterns stay sharp and clear.* 👁 *See "Scaling a Style" on page 9.*

Original Graphic

Wow-Gems 01*

Wow-Gems 02*

Wow-Gems 03*

Wow-Gems 04*

Wow-Gems 05*

Wow-Gems 06*

Wow-Gems 07*

Wow-Gems 08*

Wow-Gems 09*

Wow-Gems 10*

Wow-Gems 11*

Wow-Gems 12*

Wow-Gems 13*

Wow-Gems 14*

Wow-Gems 15*

Wow-Gems 16*

Wow-Gems 17*

Wow-Gems 18*

Wow-Gems 19*

Wow-Gems 20*

Plastics

The Styles in the **Wow-Plastics** set imitate various kinds of plastics, some opaque and others translucent. The colors are integrated into the Styles, so the original color of the type or graphic doesn't affect the final result. Most of the **Wow-Plastics** are smooth-surfaced, but four (**03, 13, 14** and **18**) are textured.

Wow-Plastics 13 and **14** are designed to work together to create the look of a sign or license plate — the black is applied to a layer with graphics or type, and the yellow is applied to the larger shape of the sign or plate in the layer underneath. 👁 *See "Type & Graphics Gallery" on page 50 for a layered sign example.*

The effects shown here are the results of applying the Styles to a file with a Resolution of 225 pixels/inch.

*Styles whose names include the * symbol have a built-in surface pattern or texture. If you need to scale one of these Styles to fit your file, there are certain scaling percentages that will ensure that the patterns stay sharp and clear. 👁 *See "Scaling a Style" on page 9.*

Original Graphic

Wow-Plastic 01

Wow-Plastic 02

Wow-Plastic 03*

Wow-Plastic 04

Wow-Plastic 05*

Wow-Plastic 06

Wow-Plastic 07

Wow-Plastic 08

Wow-Plastic 09

Wow-Plastic 10

Wow-Plastic 11

Wow-Plastic 12

Wow-Plastic 13*

Wow-Plastic 14*

Wow-Plastic 15

Wow-Plastic 16

Wow-Plastic 17

Wow-Plastic 18*

Wow-Plastic 19

Wow-Plastic 20

Polished & Textured Woods

The Layer Styles in the **Wow-Woods** set provide the look of wood — common or exotic, raw or polished, or even encased in resin. In some the wood surfaces are smooth, while in others the grain is raised.

👁 *See "Scaling a Style" on page 9 for the relationship between Layer Styles and the Resolution setting.*

*The names of all the Styles in the **Wow-Woods** set include the * symbol, which indicates that a surface pattern or texture is part of the Style. If you need to scale one of these Styles to fit your file, there are certain scaling percentages that will ensure that the patterns stay sharp and clear.* 👁 *See "Scaling a Style" on page 9.*

Original Graphic

Wow-Woods 01*

Wow-Woods 02*

Wow-Woods 03*

Wow-Woods 04*

Wow-Woods 05*

Wow-Woods 06*

Wow-Woods 07*

Wow-Woods 08*

Wow-Woods 09*

Wow-Woods 10*

Wow-Woods 11*

Wow-Woods 12*

Wow-Woods 13*

Wow-Woods 14*

Wow-Woods 15*

Wow-Woods 16*

Wow-Woods 17*

Wow-Woods 18*

Wow-Woods 19*

Wow-Woods 20*

POLISHED & TEXTURED WOODS **63**

Rock, Brick & Other Materials

The Layer Styles in the **Wow-Rocks** set were designed to endow type and graphics with the textures of everything from alien minerals (**07** is molten Kryptonite) to a variety of building materials — from bricks (**01**) to rough and smooth stone (including sandstone, **20**), and even various kinds of weathered ores (**11, 13, 16,** and **19**).

The effects shown here are the results of applying the Styles to a file with a Resolution setting of 225 pixels/inch.  See "Scaling a Style" on page 9 for the relationship between Layer Styles and the Resolution setting.

* *The names of all the Styles in the **Wow-Rocks** set include the * symbol, which indicates that a surface pattern or texture is part of the Style. If you need to scale one of these Styles to fit your file, there are certain scaling percentages that will ensure that the patterns stay sharp and clear.* See *"Scaling a Style" on page 9.*

Original Graphic

Wow-Rocks 01*

Wow-Rocks 02*

Wow-Rocks 03*

Wow-Rocks 04*

Wow-Rocks 05*

Wow-Rocks 06*

Wow-Rocks 07*

Wow-Rocks 08*

Wow-Rocks 09*

Wow-Rocks 10*

Wow-Rocks 11*

Wow-Rocks 12*

Wow-Rocks 13*

Wow-Rocks 14*

Wow-Rocks 15*

Wow-Rocks 16*

Wow-Rocks 17*

Wow-Rocks 18*

Wow-Rocks 19*

Wow-Rocks 20*

Organic Patterns

The Layer Styles in the **Wow-Organics** are seamlessly wrapping photographic patterns and textures, great for backgrounds, panels, or special fills for display text or graphics. Most of the **Wow-Organics** have shadows, bevels, or subtly embossed surface textures, so these Styles can be used to turn type or graphics into dimensional objects. But these attributes can also be turned off when you simply want a background or fill. 👁 *See the tip on page 68 for changing dimensional effects from a Style.*

The relatively large and detailed **00–03** are designed for backgrounds. **Organics 04** and **05** include stroked edges and inner shadows that make them ideal for type. Style **06** shows the brush work of coarse stucco. Styles **07, 08,** and **17–20** are woven materials whose patterns are enhanced with texture. **Organics 09–12** are papers, **13** is a corroded surface with stark outlining, **14** is cork, and **15** and **16** are bamboo variations.

Wow-Organics 00*

Wow-Organics 01*

Wow-Organics 02*

Wow-Organics 03*

Wow-Organics 04*

Wow-Organics 05*

Wow-Organics 06*

Wow-Organics 07*

Wow-Organics 08*

The names of all the **Wow-Organics Styles include the * symbol, indicating a built-in surface pattern or texture. If you need to scale one of these Styles to fit your file, there are certain scaling percentages that will ensure that the patterns stay sharp and clear.* 👁 *See "Scaling a Style" on page 9.*

Wow-Organics 09*

Wow-Organics 10*

Wow-Organics 11*

Wow-Organics 12*

Wow-Organics 13*

Wow-Organics 14*

Wow-Organics 15*

Wow-Organics 16*

Wow-Organics 17*

Wow-Organics 18*

Wow-Organics 19*

Wow-Organics 20*

Patterns & Fabrics

The Layer Styles in the **Wow-Fabric** library are seamlessly repeating patterns. The patterns are also subtly embossed on the surface, the edges are beveled, and drop shadows have been added so that these Styles can be used to turn type or graphics into dimensional objects. But these attributes can also be turned off if what you need is simply a pattern to use as a background or fill.

▶ *To change or remove the dimensional Bevel effect in a Style you've applied, simply double-click the 𝑓 icon for the "styled" layer in the Layers palette, then find Bevel Size in the list in the Style Settings dialog box and change the settings to taste. A setting of 0 effectively removes the dimensional effect of the Style leaving behind the pattern and shadow.*

▶ *The 21 Patterns used in the **WowPSE2-Fabric Patterns** Styles, plus 24 more Patterns, can be found in the **WowPSE2-Fabric Patterns** library.*

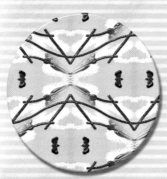
Wow-Fabric 00*

Wow-Fabric 01*

Wow-Fabric 02*

Wow-Fabric 03*

Wow-Fabric 04*

Wow-Fabric 05*

Wow-Fabric 06* **Wow-Fabric 07*** **Wow-Fabric 08***

*The names of all the Styles in the **Wow-Fabric** library include the * symbol, which indicates that a pattern is part of the Style. If you need to scale one of these Styles to fit your file, there are certain scaling percentages that will ensure that the patterns stay sharp and clear.*

👁 See "Scaling a Style" on page 9.

Wow-Fabric 09*

Wow-Fabric 10 *

Wow-Fabric 11*

Wow-Fabric 12*

Wow-Fabric 13*

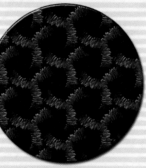

Wow-Fabric 14*

Wow-Fabric 15*

Wow-Fabric 16*

Wow-Fabric 17*

Wow-Fabric 18*

Wow-Fabric 19*

Wow-Fabric 20*

Strokes & Fills

The Layer Styles in the **Wow-Stroke** library provide everything from a simple outline, to beveled edging with a color fill, to fill treatments that look abstract or hand-painted. Some have drop shadows to "pop" the type or graphic off the page.

Styles **02**, **04**, and **05** use the color of the original graphic. Styles **03** and **18–20** can make great "comic book" headlines. Styles **09–15** provide more sophisticated colors as well as subtle interior "halos," textures and gradients. Stroke **16's** "watercolor" fill can enhance calligraphy or rough graphics. And the "crayon rubbing" fill of **17** follows the contours of the type or graphic.

Original Graphic   **Wow-Stroke 01***   **Wow-Stroke 02**

Wow-Stroke 03   **Wow-Stroke 04**   **Wow-Stroke 05**

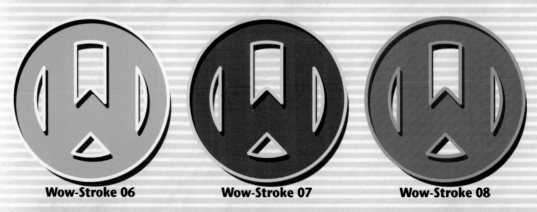

Wow-Stroke 06   **Wow-Stroke 07**   **Wow-Stroke 08**

*Styles whose names include the * symbol have a built-in surface pattern or texture. If you need to scale one of these Styles to fit your file, there are certain scaling percentages that will ensure that the patterns stay sharp and clear. 👁 See "Scaling a Style" on page 9.

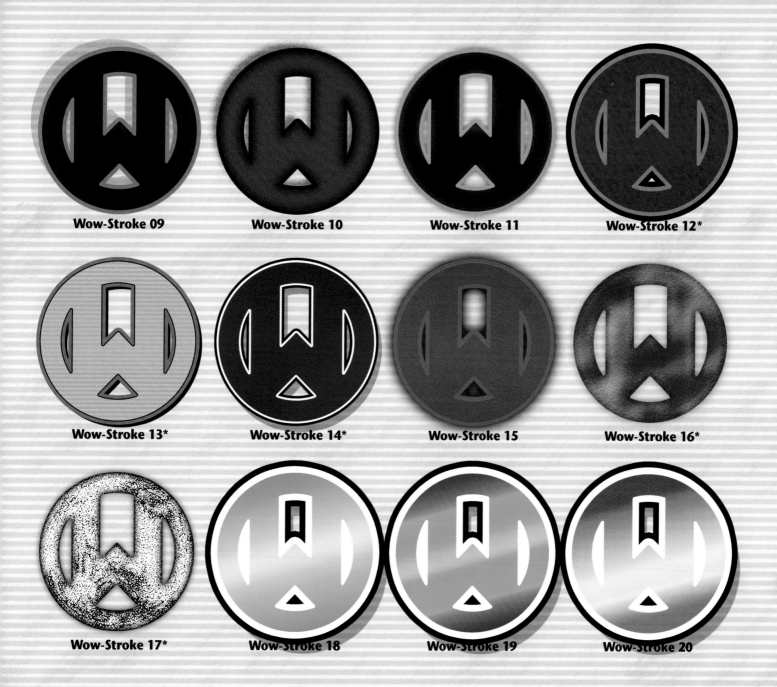

Wow-Stroke 09

Wow-Stroke 10

Wow-Stroke 11

Wow-Stroke 12*

Wow-Stroke 13*

Wow-Stroke 14*

Wow-Stroke 15

Wow-Stroke 16*

Wow-Stroke 17*

Wow-Stroke 18

Wow-Stroke 19

Wow-Stroke 20

Shadows, Halos & Embossing

Many of the **Wow-Halo** Styles are "positive and negative" pairs. So you'll find, side by side on these pages, two versions of the same general Style — one dark and one light, or one raised above the surface and one impressed into it. Shown here are the results of applying the Styles to a file with a Resolution setting of 225 pixels/inch.

The simple halos (**03** and **04**) and the rainbow Styles (**15** and **16**) keep the original fill color (here 50% gray). (The rainbows work well against "middle-tone" backgrounds rather than pure black or white.) The "noisy" halos (**05** and **06** as well as **13** and **14**) replace the original color with black and white. In all the other **Wow-Halos** the original type or graphic disappears, and the shape is defined by the halo, shadow, or embossed edge.

Styles **09** and **10** are sharp-edged and rounded versions of carved effects. **Halo 11** is a sharply embossed stamp effect, and **Halo 12** is a subtle raised emboss treatment.

Original Graphic Wow-Halo 01 Wow-Halo 02

Wow-Halo 03 Wow-Halo 04 Wow-Halo 05

Wow-Halo 06 Wow-Halo 07 Wow-Halo 08

Wow-Halo 09

Wow-Halo 10

Wow-Halo 11

Wow-Halo 12

Wow-Halo 13

Wow-Halo 14

Wow-Halo 15

Wow-Halo 16

Wow-Halo 17

Wow-Halo 18

Wow-Halo 19

Wow-Halo 20

Glows & Neons

Most of the **Wow-Glows** work best when you apply them to type or graphics used against dark or middle-tone backgrounds that contrast with their glowing light. Shown here are the results of applying the Styles to a file with a Resolution setting of 225 pixels/inch.

The multicolor glows (**18–20**) keep the original fill color of the graphic, while all the other **Wow-Glows** Styles replace the original color with the colors shown here.

Styles **03–05** are the "off" versions of the "lit" neons created by **06–08**. In these and other neons (**10–12** and **17**), the fill of the type or graphic is eliminated, and the edges are traced with "neon tubes."

You can use **Glows 09** to turn type and graphics into a glowing "plasma field," or **13–16** to make them "burn."

Original Graphic

Wow-Glows 01

Wow-Glows 02

Wow-Glows 03

Wow-Glows 04

Wow-Glows 05

Wow-Glows 06

Wow-Glows 07

Wow-Glows 08

Wow-Glows 09

Wow-Glows 10

Wow-Glows 11

Wow-Glows 12

Wow-Glows 13

Wow-Glows 14

Wow-Glows 15

Wow-Glows 16

Wow-Glows 17

Wow-Glows 18

Wow-Glows 19

Wow-Glows 20

Button Styles

The **Wow-Button** Styles were designed to look good when applied to small on-screen navigational elements created at 72 pixels/inch. As shown to the right, the **WowPSE2-20 Button Styles** are made up of sets of three similar, but distinct, Styles designed especially for the **Normal, Over,** and **Down** states of buttons. You can apply them to individual button graphics you have created in Photoshop Elements.

The top three rows of Styles in each column (**01–03, 11–13, 21–23, 31–33,** and **41–43**) are color variations of five basic Styles.

Most of the **Wow-Button** Styles replace the original color. But Style **09** retains the underlying color of the graphic or photo (in this case red), while **15** allows the color of the background to show through.

And, like any Layer Style, all these 150 **Wow-Button** Styles work great on any graphic or text — not just buttons!

Below, the **Wow Button 02-Normal** Style was applied to the **A**, the **Wow Button 40-Over** was used on the **B** and **Wow Button 05-Down** was used on the **C**. All the Styles were scaled to fit the type.

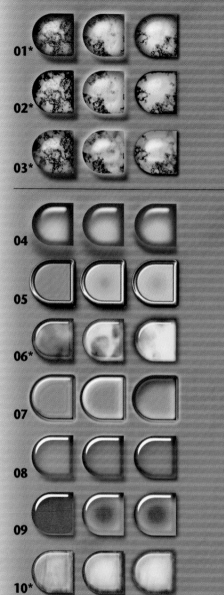
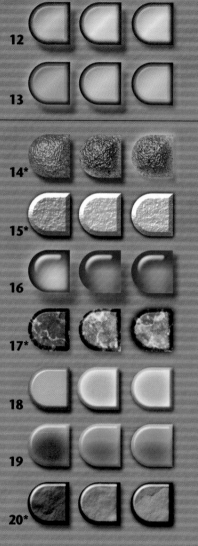

*Styles whose names include the * symbol have a built-in surface pattern or texture. If you need to scale one of these Styles to fit your file, there are certain scaling percentages that will ensure that the patterns stay sharp and clear. See "Scaling a Style" on page 9 for help.*

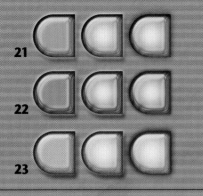

21

22

23

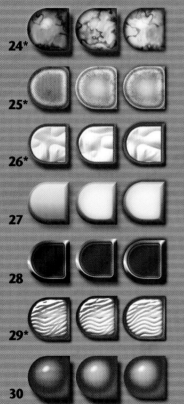

24*

25*

26*

27

28

29*

30

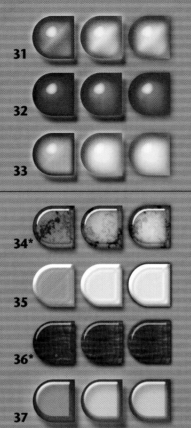

31

32

33

34*

35

36*

37

38

39

40

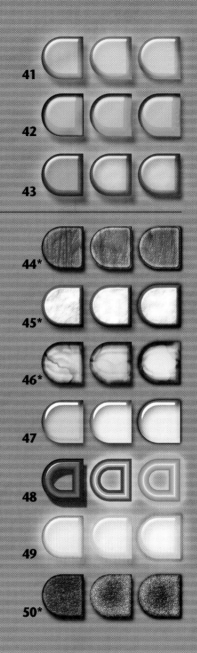

41

42

43

44*

45*

46*

47

48

49

50*

Other Wow! Presets

4

The world of **One-Click Wow!** holds a lot more than just Styles — from natural media brushes to elaborate repeating patterns to custom gradient effects, all done with Adobe Photoshop Elements 2 presets. If you followed the instructions on page 2, you'll find these **Wow Presets** throughout your Photoshop Elements menus:

- When you have any of the painting tools selected in Elements, you'll find all the **WowPSE2-Media Brushes** waiting for you in the pop-out menu of the **Options Bar** (see left). There you'll see 27 different brushes, organized into 7 "families," for simulating traditional artists' media: Chalk, Dry Brush, Oil, Pastel, Sponge, Stipple, and Watercolor. See pages 79–87 for instructions and samples of these Presets for use with the Pattern Stamp — Photoshop Element's most powerful tool for turning photograph memories into masterpieces.

- There are six sets of **Wow Patterns** for printed **Fabric**, **Marble**, **Media** substrates, **Surfaces**, **Noise** (which can be used for artistic treatments or to simulate film grain), and **Organic** materials such as wood and woven fibers. The **Wow Patterns** will be available from the pop-out menu anywhere the Patterns palette occurs; for instance, in the Fill dialog box (opened by choosing Edit > Fill), in the Pattern Fill dialog (opened when you click the "Create new fill or adjustment layer" button at the bottom of the Layers palette) and in the Options bar for the Pattern Stamp or Paint Bucket tool. See pages 86–87 for samples of the **Wow Pattern** sets.

- The **Wow Gradients** can be useful for filling type or graphics, or even for creating a background element. You can apply them with the **Gradient tool** or use them to create **Gradient Fill layers**, with all their customizable settings, such as gradient style, angle, and scale. Using the **Wow Gradients** is described on page 88–89.

When you're ready to upgrade to the full version of Photoshop and you would like more extensive step-by-step techniques for painting, making and using Patterns and Gradients, see the latest version of The Photoshop Wow! Book *(Peachpit Press).*

Thick Heavy Brushes
Wet Media Brushes
✔ WowPSE2-Media Brushes

Brushes: WowPSE2-Media Brus...

75	Wow-Chalk-Large
50	Wow-Chalk-Medium
36	Wow-Chalk-Small
10	Wow-Chalk-X Small
90	Wow-Dry Brush-Large
60	Wow-Dry Brush-Medium
30	Wow-Dry Brush-Small
10	Wow-Dry Brush-X Small
99	Wow-Oil- X Large
60	Wow-Oil-Large
35	Wow-Oil-Medium
15	Wow-Oil-Small
9	Wow-Oil-X Small
50	Wow-Pastel-Large
30	Wow-Pastel-Medium
14	Wow-Pastel-Small
60	Wow-Sponge-Large
20	Wow-Sponge-Medium
10	Wow-Sponge-Small
50	Wow-Stipple-Large
25	Wow-Stipple-Medium
20	Wow-Stipple-Small
10	Wow-Stipple-X Small
100	Wow-Watercolor-Large
60	Wow-Watercolor-Medium
25	Wow-Watercolor-Small
10	Wow-Watercolor-X Small

HOW TO PAINT WITH THE WOW MEDIA BRUSH PRESETS

Turn an existing photo into a painting with the Wow Media Brushes and Element's Pattern Stamp Tool. Or start with a blank canvas and paint from scratch with the Wow Media Brushes and the "regular" Brush Tool. Either way, you are in for some very serious creative fun.

There are two primary ways of using the **Wow Media Brushes**–for cloning a source photo into a "faux" natural media painting or drawing, or use them by selecting the "regular" **Brush Tool** and simply starting with a blank canvas and "going for it."

To create a painting from an image, start with Element's **Pattern Stamp** (with its Impressionist option), because it's the one tool that can pull just the color from a source image as you paint stroke-by-stroke without painting the detail. With the **Pattern Stamp** and the **Wow Media Brushes** you can turn a photo into a painting in five easy-to-understand steps.

Before you start, be sure the **Wow Presets** have been installed. 👁 *See page 2 if you need instructions.*

1 Preparing the photo. Choose the photo you want to turn into a painting. Save a copy of the file under a new name (**File > Save As**) so you'll have the original if you need to go back to it.

*This landscape was chosen as the basis for the cloned painting to be made with **Wow Watercolor** brushes.*

Then make any changes that you like to the copy. For instance:

- Exaggerate its color and contrast if you like, until you have the colors you want in your painting.

After the image was cropped, the contrast was increased and the color exaggerated using Levels and Hue/Saturation adjustments.

- If you want your painting to have an "unfinished edges" look, make a selection of the edges with the Marquee Tool and fill it with white (or black, or any other color that you want to use as a background). 👁 *See pages 82–83 for several examples of paintings done this way.*

2 Loading "paint" into the brush. To make the image the source for painting with the **Wow Media Brush** Presets, define it as a Pattern by choosing Edit > Define Pattern; everything that's visible will become a Pattern tile.

In the Pattern Name dialog box, type in a name and click "OK."

Now make this new Pattern the cloning source for the painting: **Choose the Pattern Stamp** from the Tools palette and **choose your new pattern** from the pop-out menu of Pattern swatches in the tool's Options bar. Also while you are there, make sure to check the Impressionist option. This feature is what allows you to pull the color, but not the detail, from your newly created source pattern.

Choosing the Pattern Stamp; it shares a space with the Clone Stamp.

Clicking the little arrow to the right of the Pattern swatch in the Options bar opens the palette of samples so you can choose the Pattern you defined.

▶ *Using a Wacom pressure-sensitive tablet and stylus with the **Wow Media Brushes** gives you better control than using a mouse.* 👁 *See the brush stroke samples on page 81 to compare. But even if you use a mouse, you can vary the size of the brush tip by keeping your fingers on the bracket keys and toggling the brush size up and down.*

*Tapping the **[** key makes a brush tip smaller; tapping **]** enlarges the brush tip.*

▶ *Be sure to take advantage of the three to five sizes of each kind of brush provided in the **Wow Media Brushes**. Even though you can change brush tip size by using the bracket keys, you'll get much better-looking brush strokes if you start with the brush that's closest to the size you want and then enlarge or reduce it slightly with the bracket keys.*

3 Making a "canvas"/surface layer. This step will add a surface layer above your image to make a foundation for your painting and to serve as a visual barrier between your original image and the painting layer so you'll be able to see your brush strokes clearly as your painting develops. One way to do this is to click the "Create new fill or adjustment layer" button at the bottom of the Layers palette, choose Solid Color, and pick white (or black or any other color). If you added a colored border as mentioned in step 2, make sure and use the same color here. When the new layer appears in the Layers palette, reduce its Opacity.

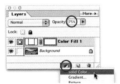

With a Color Fill layer added and its Opacity reduced, you can see your photo so it's easier to follow.

4 Preparing a paint layer and painting. Click the "Create a new layer" button at the bottom of the Layers palette to add a transparent layer for painting. Then, with the Pattern Stamp still chosen (from step 2), go to the Options Bar and choose the **WowPSE2-Media Brushes** set; then select one of the **Wow-Watercolor** brushes.

Now paint, keeping these pointers in mind:

- In general start with a larger brush and move to smaller ones as you add finer details.
- Try to paint each differently colored area separately.
- Don't "scrub" over the image, but instead make brush strokes that follow the color and shape contours.

From time to time, increase the Opacity of the Color Fill layer to hide the original image so you can see how the painting is developing.

Viewing the painting in progress, with the Opacity of the Color Fill layer at 75% (left) and at 100% (right)

After you've used the **Pattern Stamp Tool** to clone the photograph, you may want to use the same **Wow Media Brush** "family" (in this case the Wow Watercolor family) with the regular (non-cloning) **Brush Tool** and a very small brush tip, for full control as you paint the finest details. If you'd like you can choose colors for the Brush by Alt/Option-clicking existing color in your paint layer.

5 Enhancing the painting. When the painting is complete, you may want to try one of these techniques to add to it:

- Increase the density of the color by making a copy of the paint layer (**click and drag the name in the Layers palette to the New Layer icon at the bottom of the palette**). This extra layer will build up any

*The **Wow Watercolor** painting with all brush strokes completed (left) and after building up the color by duplicating the paint layer (right)*

▶ The **Wow Media Brush** presets were also designed for creating paintings from scratch, without needing to use the **Pattern Stamp Tool** and a source photograph. Of course, these brushes can also be used for adding the finishing touches to a cloned painting as well. Strokes made with the **Wow Media Brushes** and Photoshop Element's regular **Brush Tool** are shown below.

Wow-Chalk

Wow-Dry Brush

Wow-Oil

Wow-Pastel

Wow-Sponge

Wow-Stipple

Wow-Watercolor

*These are examples of strokes painted with the seven kinds of **Wow Media Brushes**. In each case the top stroke was produced with the mouse and the bottom one with a Wacom Intuos tablet.*

strokes that are partially transparent, to intensify the color. If you like the result, with the duplicate (top) paint layer active, **press Ctrl/⌘-E** to merge the two paint layers together.

• To darken the edges of paint strokes (especially with faux watercolors, to imitate the pigments "pooling" along the boundaries), target the **paint layer** in the Layers palette and **duplicate it** by dragging that layer to the New Layer icon, as mentioned on the previous page. Make sure your Foreground and Background colors in the Tool Palette are set to their defaults of black and white, then choose Filter> Sketch> **Photocopy**, and set the filter's values to 24 and 1. Finally set the blending mode of the filtered layer to Color Burn, and experiment with the layer's opacity.

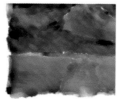

*Running the **Photocopy** filter on a duplicate of the paint layer can exaggerate color and edge detail.*

Changing the Blend Mode of the filtered layer to Color Burn (and playing with the layer's opacity) is what allows it to combine with what's below.

• Painting with the **Wow Media Brushes** creates canvas or paper texture as well as brush strokes. You can make these more apparent by applying one of the **Wow Texture Styles** to the paint layers. See examples of the **Wow Textures** on pages 44–45 and 84–85.

*Applying the **Wow-Texture 01** style to the paint layer*

• A few **Wow Styles** that are especially useful are **Texture 01**, which adds a watercolor paper overlay, **Texture 02**, for a canvas texture, **Texture 03**, which adds dimension and canvas texture to semitransparent brush strokes (good for paintings done with **Wow-Dry Brush** and **Wow-Oil**). **Texture 04** applies exaggerated gesso brush strokes and **Texture 09** will make your **Wow Watercolors** appear to have been "salt stained."

👁 *As with any layer styles, remember when you are experimenting to remove the current style before trying another one.*

▶ Here are some more tips for specifically using the **Wow Watercolor** Presets:

• *To imitate a wash, use one continuous stroke rather than starting and stopping.*

• *Don't let colors touch or the details will blur.*

• *To add density to your watercolor, duplicate the painted layer (Ctrl/⌘-J) so the partially transparent colors build, and then adjust the Opacity of this top layer to taste.*

PAINTING GALLERY

These "cloned" paintings were made using some of the **Wow-Media Brush** presets shown on pages 84–85 and the methods described on pages 79–83. They were done at various sizes and Resolution settings and reduced to fit this layout.

1 The strokes of the **Wow-Dry Brush** tools were enhanced with the **Texture 03** Style. **2 Wow-Chalk** with **Texture 07** creates the look of dry chalk on rough board. **3** This stylized illustration was converted to a painting using **Wow-Dry Brush** with **Texture 03**. **4 Wow-Watercolor** (with **Texture 01**) and **5 Wow-Chalk,** (with a black background and matching edge. See page 82) create two very different results from the same original photo. **6 Wow-Watercolor,** with its Wet Edges and Airbrush settings, was used with **Texture 09** for a wet-into-wet effect. **7** was created using the **Wow-Pastel** brushes and **Texture 06**. **8 Wow-Watercolor** (with **Texture 01**) was used with smaller brush tips than in 4. **9** The **Wow-Sponge** brush tips can create a "soft focused" effect**. 10** This loose painting on black was done using **Wow-Oil** with **Texture 03**, adding dimension to the strokes. **11** Precise brush work for fine detail was created using **Wow-Watercolor** and **Texture 01**.

6

7

8

9

10

11

Media Brush and Texture Style Presets

On these two pages are paintings made from the original photo to the right, using the **Wow Media Brush** presets, and then enhanced with some of the **Wow Texture Styles**. These paintings were produced using a Wacom Intuos tablet (for its greater control and comfort) and the five-step method outlined in "How To Paint with the Wow Media Brush Presets" on pages 79–81. The label under each picture tells which Brush set and Texture Style (if any) were used. These Styles are shown in detail on pages 44–45.

The first painted sample to the right of the Original Photograph was "hand painted" using the **Wow Media Brush** presets with Photoshop Element 2's regular **Brush Tool**, and not using Element's **Pattern Stamp Tool**, as is the case with the rest of the samples shown here. Using the **Wow Media Brushes** with the **Brush Tool** gives you chances for greater personal expression (you choose the color for each stroke yourself, and paint where ever you like on the canvas), but lacks the "automation" that comes with using the colors of a source photograph as the basis for a cloned painting using the **Pattern Stamp Tool**.

Original Photograph

"Hand Painted" with Wow Chalk

Wow-Chalk on white + Texture 07

Wow-Chalk on black + Texture 07

Wow-Dry Brush + Texture 02

Wow-Oil + Texture 02

Wow-Pastel + Texture 05

Wow-Sponge + Texture 08

Wow-Stipple + Texture 10

Wow-Watercolor + Texture 01

PATTERNS SAMPLER

Adobe Photoshop Elements 2 One-Click Wow! also comes with a set of over 150 different seamlessly repeating Patterns, organized into seven different libraries. A random sampling of 36 of these different Patterns is shown on these two pages.

The categories of these different **Wow Patterns** include: **Fabric Patterns;** a collection of retro and tropical repeats, **Marble Patterns;** a series of polished tiles, **Media Patterns;** paper and canvas textures for backgrounds or overlays, **Noise Patterns;** especially good for mezzotint effects, **Organic Patterns;** a collection woven and handmade surfaces, and **Surface Patterns;** a miscellaneous set of abstracts and synthetic materials.

Here are just a couple of the many ways that these **Wow Patterns** can be used. First, as a foundation for some layered collage project. To do this simply create a Pattern Fill layer by selecting that option from the "Create a new fill or adjustment layer" icon/menu ⊘ at the bottom of the layer palette **A**, then select a general category of **WowPSE2 Patterns** from the pop out menus **B** and **C**, then select a specific one from the resulting list **B**. While this

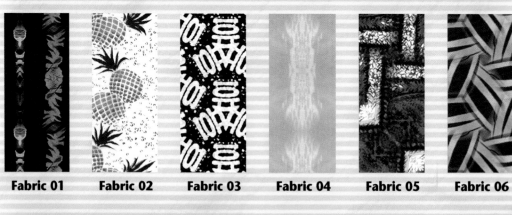

| Fabric 01 | Fabric 02 | Fabric 03 | Fabric 04 | Fabric 05 | Fabric 06 |

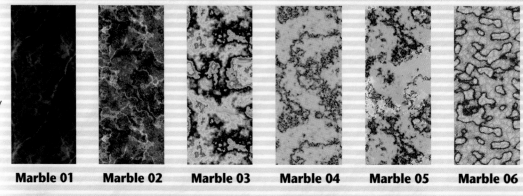

| Marble 01 | Marble 02 | Marble 03 | Marble 04 | Marble 05 | Marble 06 |

| Media 01 | Media 02 | Media 03 | Media 04 | Media 05 | Media 08 |

dialog box is open you can move your cursor into the document window and click and drag to reposition the pattern.

A second way to use a **Wow Pattern** is as an overlay. Many of the Wow Styles already have these custom patterns integrated in them, but by applying the patterns as a separate layer yourself, you will gain an additional level of control. To use a pattern as an overlay, first create a **Pattern Fill layer** above your background layer **D** as just described **E**, then simply change the Blending Mode **F** of the layer to Overlay (or have fun experimenting with other Blend Modes).

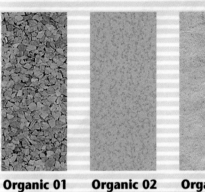

Noise 09   **Noise 10**   **Noise 11**   **Noise 12**   **Noise 13**   **Noise 14**

Organic 01   **Organic 02**   **Organic 03**   **Organic 04**   **Organic 09**   **Organic 14**

Surface 01   **Surface 02**   **Surface 03**   **Surface 05**   **Surface 09**   **Surface 26**

GRADIENT EFFECTS

The **Wow-Gradients** can be useful for filling type or graphics, or even for creating a background element. Three of the "rainbow" gradients (**04, 05,** and **06**) create transparent top and bottom edges to allow part of the background to show through.

You can apply them with the **Gradient tool** or use them to create **Gradient Fill layers**, with all their customizable settings, such as gradient style, angle, and scale.

To create a Gradient Fill layer, click on the "Create a new fill or adjustment layer" icon at the bottom of the layer palette, then choose Gradient, then select the **Wow PSE2-Gradients** from the pop out menus **A**, and select a specific one. While this dialog box is open, you can move your cursor into the document window and click and drag to reposition the gradient. Double click on the layer icon **B** at any time to change the settings.

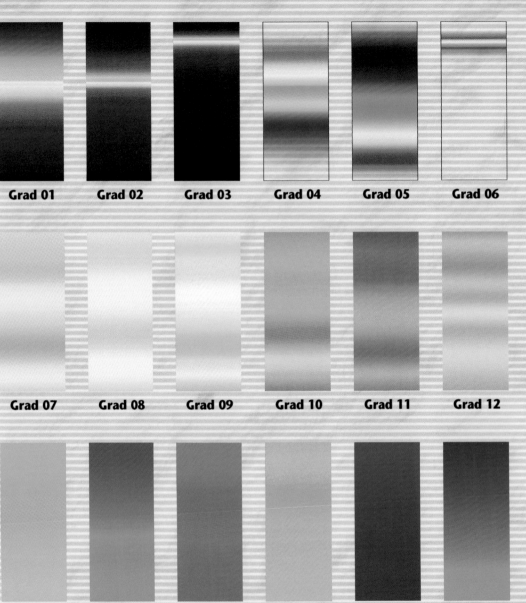

Grad 01   Grad 02   Grad 03   Grad 04   Grad 05   Grad 06

Grad 07   Grad 08   Grad 09   Grad 10   Grad 11   Grad 12

Grad 13   Grad 14   Grad 15   Grad 16   Grad 17   Grad 18